THE INDEPENDENT GUIDE TO
PARIS 2016
2nd EDITION

Limit of Liability and Disclaimer of Warranty:
The publisher has used its best efforts in preparing this book, and the information provided herein is provided "as is." Independent Guides and the author make no representation or warranties with respect to the accuracy or completeness of the contents of this book and specifically disclaims any implied warranties of merchantability or fitness for any particular purpose and shall in no event be liable for any loss of profit or any other commercial damage, including but not limited to special, incidental, consequential, or other damages.
Please read all signs before entering attractions, as well as the terms and conditions of any third party companies used. Prices are approximate, and do fluctuate.

Table of Contents:

Welcome to Paris

We would like to begin with a big "thank you" for purchasing The Independent Guide to Paris 2016. This guide includes all sorts of information that will enhance your visit to the "City of Lights". You will learn the transport system, find out the multitude of ways of getting to the city, get an insight into local customs, learn about where to stay, discover where to dine, have a look at all the main attractions, and much more. This guide aims to be easy to read and concise, yet comprehensive, covering every aspect of your trip to Paris.

There is no advertising in this guide - it is completely independent and we have not been paid for any of these opinions by any company mentioned herein.

If you have any questions about the guide please contact us using our contact form at www.independentguidebooks.com.

A Brief History

Paris has an interesting past that has shaped the city, its people and their customs. To get an idea of why the city is the way it is today, *Independent Guides* presents a brief history.

Bastille's revolution

The French Revolution began in 1789 and ended in 1790, with the ascent of Napoleon Bonaparte. During this period, French citizens redesigned their country's political landscape, erasing centuries-old institutions such as the absolute monarchy.

The Bastille was originally constructed in 1370 as a fort to protect the walled city of Paris from English attack. It was later made into an independent stronghold, and its name "bastide" slowly became Bastille. **The Bastille** was first used as a state prison in the 17th century, and its cells were reserved for upper class criminals, political troublemakers, and spies. Most prisoners there were imprisoned without a trial under direct orders of the king. Standing 100 feet tall and surrounded by a moat more than 80 feet wide, the Bastille was an imposing structure in the Parisian landscape.

On 14 July 1789, Parisians took siege of the Bastille fortress. This event was the start of the French Revolution and the decline of the divine right of monarchs in France. On 17 July, the national tricolour flag with the colours of Paris (blue and red) and of the King (white) was adopted at the **Hôtel de Ville** by Louis XV.

Louis XVI and Queen Marie-Antoinette, royals at the time, were executed on the **Place de la Concorde**. The Reign of Terror took hold. By order of the new revolutionary government, the Bastille was torn down. Today, July 14 Bastille Day is celebrated as a national holiday in France.

Napoleon

Napoleon Bonaparte, with a "coup d'état" overthrew the French Directory (the government at the time) and put an end to the Revolution.

Napoleon was crowned emperor in **Notre Dame Cathedral** in 1804. During his reign, Napoleon shaped the city and developed it in many ways. He gave Paris the **Ourcq canal**, the embankments, the creation of the sewerage system and the **Arc de Triomphe**.

It is one of the most famous monuments in Paris. It stands in the centre of the **Place de l'Etoile**, at the western end of the **Champs-Elysées**. The Arc de Triomphe, honours those who fought and died for France in the French Revolutionary and the Napoleonic Wars. Its design was inspired by the Roman Arch of Titus.

In 1852 during the second republic, the capital was transformed thanks to Prefect Haussmann. He doubled the width of traffic lanes and made pavements commonplace, making walking around the city an easy affair. He also created 2,000 hectares of woodland and planted 90,000 trees along major roads. He developed a 500-km-long sewerage network. Paris' five mainline railway stations were completed in 1847.

The city of Paris and railway companies were also thinking about the construction of an urban railway system to link inner districts of the city. The need was real because the urban transport network consisted primarily of a large number of omnibus lines prior to 1845. Many projects were proposed but finally, on 20 April 1896, Paris adopted the Fulgence Bienvenüe project, which was to serve only the centre of Paris.

Unlike many other subway systems, such as that of London, this system was designed with nine lines from the outset. The construction began in November 1898 and the first metro line was inaugurated un July 1900 during the Paris World's Fair.

Then came Paris at war...

During WWI, the battle of the Marne saved Paris from the Germans, but the city could not escape the fate of WWII.

A collaborationist state was established in Vichy (in central France), governed by Marshal Petain. In 1942, 12,000 Jews were arrested and gathered together at the Vélodrome d'Hiver to be deported. Paris was liberated on 25 August 1944. The following day, General de Gaulle paraded down the Champs-Élysées. The city was saved: the German commander Dietrich von Choltitz, in charge of defence in Paris, disobeyed Hitler's order to demolish the capital's historic buildings.

Paris as we know it today, with all of its beautiful monuments, was completed in the 1960s. In the 1970s, the Paris ring road, the **Montparnasse Tower** and the **Palais des Congrès** convention centre were completed. Many important buildings have flourished since: the **Opera Bastille**, the **Grande Arche de la Défense**, and the **Stade de France** to name but a few.

Architectural changes

In the early 1950s, the 1960s and the 1970s, Paris' urban landscape changed as high buildings began to dominate the skyline. The architectural evolution of Paris is similar to French cities. In the 1950s it was about massive towers, whereas in the 1960s modern elaborate buildings emerged such as "Unesco ", and "Maison de la Radio". Architecture at this point was no longer an art but an industry.

In 1968 the renovation of **Hauts-de-Belleville** and **Italy** began. Both led to the disappearance of the older districts, replaced by tower blocks to increase the amount of accommodation.

Alongside the so-called "destruction-reconstruction", the old districts gained value. We have to wait until 1974 to see the attempt to improve the liveability of the city as the city began to think about the preservation of parks, gardens and pathways. The 1980s marked a return to classic templates from Haussmann such as the alignment of buildings on the street. However, this "post-modernism" remains faithful to the pure and cubic volumes of modern architecture.

The presidents of the Fifth Republic also left their mark on the urban landscape of the capital, President **Pompidou**, for example, created the eponymous **Cultural Centre**.

In April 1973, Paris' road users got a major improvement with the inauguration of the city's ring road. 17 years after the beginning of the work and 13 years after opening the first section, motorists could finally go around Paris in a mere 35km. Town planners were against the project, but President Pompidou simply remarked, "the French people love cars."

The years 1980-1990 were marked by François Mitterrand and his program, imposing buildings often inspired by pure geometric forms: the **Arche de la Défense**, the **Louvre pyramid**, the **Opera Bastille**, and the **Ministry of Economy and Finance** in Bercy all came to be.

Introducing Paris: The City of Light

The capital of France, Paris is a large city of 105km², and home to over 2 million people *intra-muros* (an area that once would have been marked by a fortress-style wall). The city of Paris and its numerous suburbs is called Ile de France, and with a total population of 12 million constitutes the hub of French economic life.

Currency:

The currency in use in Paris, as in a large part of Europe, is the Euro (EUR). Note that travellers cheques, as well as cheques in general, are no longer accepted in the vast majority of establishments. As such, a mix of cash and card is recommended. We recommend using a pre-paid card or using a no-fee debit card from your home country. For UK users we recommend FairFx's pre-paid debit card service. There is usually a £9.95 fee for the card but by using our exclusive link you get the card for free: **http://bit.ly/debitdlp**. Cash bonuses are also available for top-ups of over £250.

Visa and Mastercard are the most widely accepted brands of credit and debit cards, with Maestro and American Express being accepted at select establishments. In Europe, the Chip and Pin system is used and as such waiters and shop assistant will be unfamiliar with the signature system used in certain countries, such as the USA. Some may refuse signature card payments altogether.

The structure of the city:

Paris is divided in 20 areas (or regions) called "arrondissements". Each arrondissement is governed separately by a local mayor. The overall city is managed by the Mayor of Paris who supervises each municipality and has a more general view of the city. Arrondissement number 1 is in the city centre, and these increase sequentially outwards in a spiral shape. See the image on the next page.

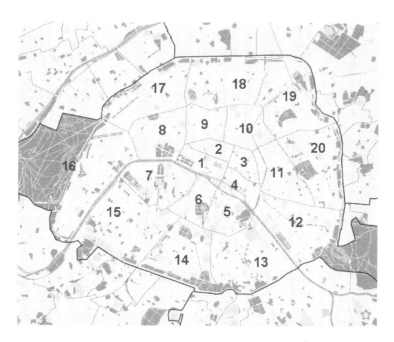

List of arrondissements:

No.	District	No.	District
1	Le Louvre	11	Popincourt
2	La Bourse	12	Reuilly
3	Le Temple	13	Les Gobelins
4	L'Hôtel de Ville	14	L'Observatoire
5	Le Panthéon	15	Vaugirard
6	Le Luxembourg	16	Passy
7	Le Palais Bourbon	17	Les Batignolles-Monceau
8	L'Elysée	18	La Butte Montmartre
9	L'Opéra	19	Les Buttes Chaumont
10	L'Enclos Saint Laurent	20	Ménilmontant

Visiting patterns:
France is the world's most visited country according to official figures from the World Tourism Organization. Paris is most widely visited during the summer school holiday period which runs from July to August. The period from September to December is noticeably calmer as the long nights start to draw in. January to March is even less busy but temperatures are generally cold. As Spring, comes in from April to June, the weather starts to become warmer and visitors return.

Weather:
Paris enjoys an oceanic climate, with an average *minimum* temperature of 15 degrees Celsius between June and August, and 3 degrees Celsius from December to February. Average *maximums* are 25 degrees in July and August, down to 8 degrees from January to February. The key to packing for Parisian weather is layers – whereas in the middle of a summer's day the weather may reach 30 or 35 degrees Celsius, the evenings will be colder and require a light jacket.

Rainfall in Paris happens throughout the year. On average it rains between 10 to 15 days per month throughout the entire year. An umbrella is, therefore, a must regardless of when you are visiting.

Events throughout the Year:
Paris is known as one of the cultural capitals of the world and it holds dozens of events throughout the year, from music festivals to art festivals, and from expositions to pop-up beaches. Here we regroup some of the events that you simply miss during your visit.

In this section we note the most recent dates for the events. Where dates and locations are not given, it is because these were not available at the time of writing.

January:
- **Cirque de Demain** – The 'Circus of Tomorrow' showcases the best in young circus performing talent from juggling to trapeze acts to acrobatics. Usually runs on the last Thursday to Sunday of January. The next edition runs from 28th January to 31st January 2016.
- **Fête des Rois** – This religious event is focused around the 6th January which is the *fête des rois* (The Kings' Party), it is traditional to

eat a *galette des rois* around this date. These are available from all good *boulangeries* (bakers) and supermarkets.

- **Hôtel de Ville Ice Rink** – Skate in this magnificent ice rink located in beautiful central Paris. There is not cost to skate if you can provide your own skates, or €6 otherwise. You must wear gloves and some form of ID is needed for skate rental. The ice rink is generally present from mid-December to the end of February each year.
- **Prix d'Amerique** – This horse-racing event takes place at the Paris-Vincennes Hippodrome and boasts a prize of €1 million for the winning horse. The event takes place on the last Sunday of every January. The next edition runs on 31st January 2016.
- **Fashion Shows** – These run in January each year, and are usually made up of the Men's Fashion shows and Haute Couture shows. They display the season's summer collections. 2016 dates are January 20th to 24th for Men's Fashion, and January 24th to 29th for Haute Couture.

February:

- **Carnival** – The Carnival season in Paris is dominated by the street parade (*La Promenade du Boeuf Gras* – the fat cow parade) with performers wearing all kinds of glittery jewelry and costumes, face paint and masks – all accompanied by a soundtrack to get everyone in the mood. The parade will next be held on Sunday 7th February 2016.
- **Chinese New Year** – Yet another major street parade is held each year for Chinese New Year. Expect traditional music, clothing, dancers, chinese dragons and food to immerse you in the Asian atmosphere. Several events and happenings occur over a weekend each February. Check out the Chinese Quarter in the 13th arrondissement for the biggest celebrations.

March:

- **International Agriculture Show** – The Paris International Agricultural Show is the meeting place for players in the world of agriculture. It is a unique experience to see the inside workings of the agricultural world. There are over 1,000 exhibitors each year and about 4,000 animals. Explore the show's four sections: livestock breeding, culinary products, crops and plants, and agricultural services and professions. The event will next take place from Saturday 27th February to Sunday 6th March 2016.

- **Banlieu Blues** – This annual jazz festival runs every year starting roughly in mid-March to mid-April, and is based in Seine-Saint-Denis with several venues taking place. It is the place to see jazz talent from around the world in one place. Shows usually cost €10 to €20, with a *Pass Festival* being available for multiple concerts too. In 2016, the event runs from 18th March to 15th April.

April:

- **Salon des realités nouvelles** – Contemporary abstract art exhibition featuring over 400 different artists. You will find sculptures, paintings, photographs and more. The show has been held at the *Parc Floral de Paris* in Vincennes for a number of years.
- **Foire du Trône** – This huge funfair comes to the *Bois de Vincennes* every year, and provides an alternative to some of the world-class theme parks around the city. After paying admission, you must pay for each ride too, which can make the trip more expensive than you would think. From bumper cars to Ferris wheels and rollercoasters to log flumes, there is something for every age and taste here. In 2016, the event runs from 25th March to 23rd May.

May:

- **Nuit des Musées** – This European celebration allows you to enjoy some of the best museums in the country in a unique nighttime spectacular. Admission is free. Over 1300 museums in France participate in this event. All the museums you could imagine participate from the Louvre, to Orsay, and even the UNESCO headquarters in Paris. In 2016, the event takes place on 21st May.
- **Saint-Germain-des-Pres Jazz Festival** – Yet another one of Paris' jazz festivals, this one promises to enchant you. With tickets prices from as low as €8 to €20, and discounts for 3 and 5 show tickets, you can get your music fix in Saint-Germain-des-Pres. The event takes place 19th to 31st May 2016.
- **The French Open** – The renowned tennis tournament is one of the highlights of the year. Come and see world-class players battle for the top spot. The event runs from 22nd May to the first week of 5th June 2016. Tickets start at €12, and should be booked well in advance.

June:

- **Paris Gay Pride** – Every year over half a million people take to the streets of Paris for the annual Gay Pride festivities. These celebrate gay, lesbian, bisexual and trans people in a festive atmosphere. However, you can identify with any sexuality (including heterosexual) and turn up – the very nature of the event is that it is inclusive. There is a large parade every year, as well as a stage set up on *Place de la Republique* with shows in the evening. 2016 dates are not yet available.
- **Fête de la Musique** – The whole country takes part in a massive musical extravaganza every year in the *Fête de la Musique* with free concerts held in every town and city. From jazz to rap to hip-hop, and classic to pop, there is something for everyone. The event takes place on the 21st June every year, no matter which day of the week it falls on. Public transport runs throughout the night during the event, making getting around easy. The event is held on 21st June in 2016.

July:

- **Bastille Day** – This national holiday is arguably the most important one throughout the year, as Bastille Day *(La fête Nationale)* celebrates the beginning of the French Revolution that changed the country so much. You can expect a fireworks show at the Eiffel Tower, and to see the French Air Force fly overhead, as well as the military parade held in the morning. The event take place on 14th July each year.
- **Paris Plages** – The sun and sea come to Paris every year in the form of *Paris Plages*. These make-shift beaches, complete with sand and sun umbrellas, line the banks of the River Seine and provide a perfect way to relax in the summer sun. Note that swimming in the river is not permitted, however. As well as the beaches along the seine, more are available along the *Bassin de la Villette*. The event runs from mid-July to mid-August every year and is free to attend. In 2016 the event runs from 18th July to 21st August.
- **Open Air Cinema at Parc de la Villette** – This free-admission, open-air cinema event is a perfect chance to wind down the long summer nights with a movie. A deckchair can be rented for the evening for €7. All films are shown in their original language with subtitles in French. The event usually runs rom mid-July to mid-August each year; exact dates for 2016 were not available at the time of writing. Films are shown from Wednesday to Sunday each week.

August:

- **Festival Classique du Vert** – From August to mid-September, *Parc Floral de Paris* in *Bois de Vincennes* becomes home to classical music concerts. The event is often compared to the British summer proms series. Tickets here are reasonably priced at €6 per adult and €3 for under-26s. 2016 dates are not yet available, but it is expected tor run for all of August until mid-September.
- **Festival Rock en Seine** – Get ready for this pop and rock extravaganza, with a great mix of new and well-known acts. The 2015 line up includes Alt-J, The Chemical Brothers, Kasabian and Ben Howard amongst many others. Previous acts include Arctic Monkeys, Foo Fighters and Green Day to name just a few. This 3-day festival takes place on the last weekend in August of every year in the suburb of *Saint-Cloud*. Tickets are €119 for the full three days, and individual day tickets are also available. Camping for the festival is also available for a charge. 2016 dates are 26th to 28th August.

September:

- **Techno Parade** – This event is a parade of vehicles through the city centre, blasting out techno music. This is a popular event with over 350,000 spectators every year. At the time of writing, the event's location and date have not been released – this changes every year.
- **Journées du Patrimoine** – This is a unique event that allows you free access into most monuments and cultural locations through France. This means not only free access to museums, but also to governmental and national buildings that are not usually open to visitors. As well as open visits, there are guided tours, informational sessions and more, all designed to allow you to truly admire the city and its culture. This is a European-wide event. In 2016 the event will be held on the 17th and 18th September.
- **Festival d'Automne** – This contemporary arts festival allows you to enjoy performance, visual arts, music, cinema, dance and more in various locations throughout Paris. There is something here to suit everyone. A la carte tickets for each event are available, as are a variety of multi-event pass options. 2016 dates are not yet available.
- **La Villete Jazz Festival** – Jazz is the name of the game, in this yearly festival. The *Under the Radar* sub-festival features new and upcoming acts. Show tickets vary in price from €22 to €40, with multi-event tickets available, as well as other discounted tickets. 2016 dates are not yet available.

October:

- **Nuit Blanche** – This event aims lights up the night from dusk till dawn in an incredible one-night only extravaganza. Contemporary art is on display throughout the night including light displays, visual arts, and performance pieces. There are hundreds of different piece to enjoy all over the city. An event not to be missed. This event takes place on the night of the first Saturday in October. In 2016, the date is the evening and night of 1st October.

- **Salon du Chocolat** – This unique event allows you to discover and savour chocolate from around the world, with over 220 chocolatiers taking part – it is the largest event of its kind in the world. The event takes place at the Paris *Porte de Versailles* Exhibition Center and will run from 28th October to 1st November 2016. Tickets are priced at €14 for adults and €6.50 for children.

- **Prix de l'Arc de Triomphe** – Europe's most prestigious horseracing event takes place each year at the *Longchamp* racecourse in *Bois de Boulogne* with a total prize bundle on offer of over €5million. With 60,000 in-stadium spectators and a worldwide television audience of 1 billion, this is an event that horseracing fans cannot miss. The event will take place on the 1st and 2nd October 2016.

- **Mondial de l'Automobile** – The Paris auto show runs every two years at the exposition centre at *Porte de* Versailles and allows you to see the latest innovations in car technology, as well as several exhibitions with vehicles throughout time. Almost every major brand takes part in this event and over 1 million people visit the event. The 2016 Automobile event runs from 1st to 16th October. Tickets for the previous edition were priced at €14 per adult, €8 for under 26s, and free for children aged less than 10 years old – we expect the 2016 event prices to be in line with these. The event alternates with the **Salon de la Moto**, an expo about motorbikes, scooters and quad bikes. This runs during the Automobile show's years off – the next *Moto* event runs in December 2017, with ticket prices roughly the same as the Automobile show.

- **Foire International d'Art Contemporain** – This international arts festival counts over 3,000 artists every year, and is based in the magnificent *Grand Palais*, although galleries are spread out all across the city and even outdoors. The outdoor portions of the festival *(hors les murs)* are open access and free of charge. The *OFF*-extension of the Festival is based in the *Cité de la Mode et du Design* expands the offerings. Tickets are €40 for adults and €20 for those aged under 26. 2016 dates are not yet available.

November:

- **BNP Paribas Masters** – This tennis tournament is one of the most prestigious worldwide. Tickets start at €53. The event takes place from 31st October to 6th November in 2016.
- **Mois de la Photo** – Celebrate the wonder of the still picture during Paris' *Mois de la Photo* (photo month) that happens every two years. The next event will take place in November 2016.
- **Beaujolais Nouveau** – This event is named after the wine, and is the first day of the year when *beaujolais nouveau* should be uncorked. It is an artisan wine with fruity flavours, and designed to be enjoyed from the third Thursday of November onwards. Any good *bar à vin* will celebrate this occasion. This 60-year-old tradition will next be celebrated on 17th November 2016.

December:

- **Christmas Markets** – During the Christmas season there is no way you can miss the Christmas markets. These can be found all over central Paris and are made up of small huts, each with their own individual vendors selling everything from mulled wine to arts and crafts. You will find markets all along the *Avenue des Champs Elysées*, *Place du Trocadéro*, *Place de la Nation* and *Place Saint-Germain-des-Prés*.
- **Salon du Cheval** – This horse and pony show is perfect for equestrian fans. Buy accessories, talk to other horse fans, take part in conferences, see national and international competitions and much more. The event runs from 26th November to 4th December in 2016.
- **Salon Nautique International de Paris** – The Paris International Boat Show is a nautical dream with sail boats, board sports, motorboats and more under one roof. This year, the show runs from 3rd to 11th December 2016. Ticket prices had not yet been released at the time of writing but are usually about €15 per person.

Top Attractions in Paris:

For a quick guide to what you cannot miss on your trip, look no further.

1. The Eiffel Tower

This 19th century work of art was originally designed for the 1889 World's Fair and has come to be the symbol of Paris ever since. Designed, at the time, to only be a temporary addition, it is now difficult to imagine the city with it. You can climb the Eiffel Tower either by elevator or via the steps for an unrivalled view over Paris.

2. Notre-Dame de Paris

This Gothic cathedral dates back to the 12th century, although numerous additions and changes have been made over the years. Even from the outside the numerous facades are something to admire – from the West Front with the twin tower structure, to the South Rose window's depiction of Christ, to the stunning Flying Bustresses on the eastern side. Climb the North tower's 387 steps for stunning views over Paris and a closer look at the gargoyles.

3. Champs-Elysées

The *Avenue des Champs-Elysées* is a major shopping district in the heart of Paris. With extremely wide pavements, unrivalled by most other European cities, this place is a shopper's paradise – from luxury brands to high street retail, small cafes to large superstores. The *Champs-Elysées* is a true reflection of the international epicentre that Paris has become. Numerous parks run alongside this major thoroughfare. Be sure to check out the nearby *Palais de l'Elysée* on *Rue St-Honoré*, the official residence of the French president, as well as the *Grand* and *Petit Palais* which are both also located here.

4. Sacré-Coeur

Located a bit further out than most Parisian attractions, the Sacré-Coeur is a Catholic basilica in Montmartre that stands on the highest point in the city giving you a beautiful view. It really is worth making the short trip to the basilica to admire both the church itself (unveiled in the early 20th century) and the view of the city. Make sure to climb up to the dome too.

5. Musée d'Orsay

Housed inside an old train station, the *Musée d'Orsay* is the other must-do museum in the city, after *The Louvre*. The museum is mainly home to French art and includes works from Monet, Van Gogh and Manet to name but a few. Delacroix's *The Lion Hunt* and James McNeill Whistler's *Whistler's Mother* are particular highlights not to be missed.

6. Arc de Triomphe

One of Paris' most famous monuments, The *Arc de Triomphe* is located in the centre of one of Paris' busiest roundabouts. The Arch remembers the war-dead from the Napoleonic and French Revolutionary Wars – it stands 50 metres tall. Underneath the arch lies the *Tomb of the Unknown Soldier*. The interior of the arch houses a museum which details the design and construction of the arch. You can also climb to the top for a panoramic view of Paris.

7. Centre Pompidou

This imposing structure, with its unique futuristic design, is a cultural centre that is most famous for the Modern and Contemporary art museum located inside it. As well as the modern art museum, there is a café, a shop, as well as the Public Information library, and IRCAM where music and acoustic research takes place.

8. Jardin du Luxembourg

This public park is a beautiful place to come and enjoy the sunshine, or walk through on an autumn's evening. Set against the backdrop of the Luxembourg Palace, it is famous for its immaculate flowerbeds, traditional sailboats and the Medici Fountain. There are over 100 statues to admire in the park, including a small replica of the Statue of Liberty, and the beautiful *Fontaine de l'Observatoire*.

9. Sainte-Chapelle

The *Sainte-Chapelle* is undoubtedly one of the jewels of Paris. The Gothic chapel will mesmerise you from the moment you step inside, and you can spend hours just getting lost in the amazing depictions of biblical scenes in the 13th-century stained glass windows. Along with the *Conciergerie*, located just moments away, these are the only original remnants of the stunning palace that once stood on the site. The *Sainte-Chapelle* has only recently reopened, in May 2015, after a lengthy refurbishment.

10. Musée du Louvre

Instantly recognisable from the glass pyramid outside, the *Louvre* is the world's most visited museum, and also one of the largest. On display are over 35,000 individual artefacts and a full day is needed at this museum to really appreciate the collection. Those looking for the world-renowned "Mosa Lisa" (La Joconde) will be pleased to find it on display here.

Customs and Useful Tips

One of the ways to truly integrate into a city's culture is to understand its customs. France, and Paris, like everywhere else in the world has its own particular set of customs which when followed can lead to an enlightening experience.

Greetings and Manners

Good manners are extremely important to the French and the lack of these will make your visit much more difficult than it needs to be. There is no better way to annoy a French person than to forget a few basic phrases.

When walking into any establishment, be it a shop, restaurant, café, hotel, taxi, or when in contact with anyone who works in customer service, the first word that should come out of your mouth during a conversation is *"Bonjour"* (Hello) or alternatively *"Bonsoir"* (Hello/Good evening). This is perhaps, singlehandedly, the most important word in any French conservation. If you wish, this can be followed by *"Excusez moi,"* (Excuse me). You should *never* start a conversation by simply asking a question directly.

Side note: It is not uncommon, either, for people to utter a general "Bonjour" when walking into a small shop.

If you want to ask someone whether they speak English *"Parlez-vous Anglais?"* is the phrase to use.

"S'il vous plaît" (please) and *"Merci"* (Thank you) are also important during a conversation. You will find that the cold Parisian façade soon disappears with just a few pleasantries.

If you are talking to someone who you do not know, you should make sure to use the formal "vous" version of French verbs and not the "tu" version no matter the age of the person you are speaking to. Using "tu" is considered an acceptable greeting between friends but should never be used for an acquaintance or a member of staff. The exception would be when talking to very young children; here the "tu" version is acceptable.

In restaurants and cafés

Reservations: If you wish to have lunch at a particular restaurant, it is best to book your table in advance. However, if you are simply out and about and need to stop for lunch between visits, then just walk into whatever restaurant you fancy and you are very likely to find a table. For dinner, it is always best to call and reserve your table in advance.

Tipping: By law, a service fee is included in the restaurant and café prices. It is therefore not required to tip your waiter/waitress as they receive a fixed salary. Very good service should still, of course, be met with a tip (5% to 10%) even if one is already included in the price of your meal – this is because the service fee you have paid for is used to pay the waiters' salaries and does not top up their wage. The French rarely tip, unless service is exceptional.

Calling a waiter: A few years ago it was still acceptable to snap your fingers to attract a waiter's attention. Today, this is considering extremely rude, and a simple and discreet wave of your hand will do the trick.

Paying: The waiter will bring the bill to your table and you can pay cash or by credit card. Always request the portable card machine to be brought to you, or take your bill to the counter and pay there. Never take your eyes off your card, to avoid card skimming.

The menu: By law, priced menus are displayed outside of all restaurants, so you can first view them, then decide if you wish to visit the particular establishment.

Seating: When entering a restaurant, a hostess should greet you and direct you to a table. Should this not happen, feel free to take a seat at the table of your choice and call a waiter.

The "Doggy bag": Taking home your meal's leftovers is not something that is done in France.

Bring your own wine: The French are very particular about their wine, and bringing your own is not done. A wine must be matched to the meal and its various dishes, and often present to help you choose. Take this opportunity to learn about wines and wine matching. Some restaurants might allow guests to bring their own wine, but will charge a corkage fee. Check with them first.

Taxis:

Parisian taxi drivers can be very talkative and enjoy foreign visitors. They usually speak at least basic English, and will be happy to practice their language skills with you. Do not hesitate to have a conversation with them; they know Paris like no one else and can give you very useful tips and advice.

All taxis are regulated and a meter is installed in each vehicle. Make sure that the meter is reset when you get in, only the "tarif de prise en charge" should show. This is the minimum amount to take on passengers. One piece of luggage is usually free; additional items are charged for.

There are taxi ranks all over Paris, called "bornes de taxi" where taxis wait. If you cannot see one, just wait a few minutes at the rank. Should you be unable to find a taxi tank, it is not uncommon to ask for a telephone number to call one from a café.

Payments:

Credit cards are widely accepted: Visa and Mastercard are the most accepted brands. American Express, Maestro, Diners Club etc. are less widely accepted. You might be asked if you prefer your card debited in a different currency other than Euro. It is best to have your card debited in Euro in Paris, in order to minimise intermediaries, hence reducing bank charges and exchange rate risk.

Withdrawing cash: ATMs are widely available. Before you leave, check if your bank has an affiliated French bank, and if so use these bank's ATMs. All ATMs will recognise that the credit card you inserted is from another, country and will automatically switch to your language.

Traveller's Cheques: Traveller's cheques are not recommended, as it is rare for establishments to accept them directly. Should you have Traveller's cheques with you, they can be exchanged at any bank. Note that most banks are closed Saturday afternoons and Sundays. Some may additionally close on Monday mornings, if they are open on Saturday morning.

Driving in Paris:

Driving in Paris can be very challenging and stressful, but no more so than other large capital cities. If driving, please be aware that French law requires all drivers to have a reflective jacket on display in your vehicle at all times in case of an emergency. You must also carry a warning triangle and a personal breathalyser in the boot of your car.

If the car you will be driving comes from the UK, where they drive on the left, then you will also need to purchase headlight beam changers. These are stickers that you apply to your headlights and change the direction of the beam, so that they do not dazzle drivers in France. Check for any other applicable driving laws before you leave.

Please be aware that some rules like the American "turn right on red" are not used in France. If you have chosen to hire a car, choose to hire a GPS as well, in order to better anticipate and prepare your trips. And whatever you do — try and avoid the mess that is the *Arc de Triomphe* roundabout.

Taking the Métro (subway):

The Métro is the fastest, most efficient transport system in Paris. The extended network of lines and stations ensures that every single remote corner of the city is covered. Taking the Métro is easy, and the system is very user friendly.

Tickets can be bought either at the machines or at the offices at each station. The machines are simple to operate: simply choose the destination you wish to get to, and follow the on-screen instructions. These are available in several different European languages, including English.

If you are staying in Paris for a few days and are planning to take the metro a few times, various pass options are available. Enquire at the counters at any station for advice and to buy these passes. They are also available from the station machines.

The corridors in the subway are famous for their young musicians. These artists are all duly registered and authorised, and make a living out of their art. Leaving a few coins is good practice. A lot of famous French singers started in the Métro, and you might be supporting the next star. For a full guide to the transport system check out our transportation chapter.

Taking the bus:

The bus network is even larger than the subway system, and allows you to enjoy the view, as well as take you where you need to go. The bus tickets are the same as the Métro tickets (called Ticket T+), and can be bought on the bus as well at ticket machines. Bus stops have a full map of the bus network.

Personal safety:

Walking and travelling in Paris is generally safe. You should, however, use common sense and keep handbags closed, wallets in your inside pocket, and mobile phones out of sight. Do not leave any luggage or bag unattended.

Walking at night is not recommended in certain areas, (avoid the suburb of Seine-St-Denis for example, and the 18th and 19th arrondissements). It is recommended to use taxis at night time. Be aware of street scams, and beggars particularly near the larger tourist attractions. Pickpockets operate constantly in crowded areas, included visitor attractions and on the metro and buses.

Scams to be aware of include: the gold ring scam in which someone finds a 'gold' ring on the floor and tries to sell it to you at a knockdown price; the "deaf beggars" asking you to sign a petition and donate who are anything but deaf; the friendship bracelets that are tied around your finger and have to pay for; and the game where you have to guess which cup a ball is under. Be aware that any of these scams may also be distractions to pickpocket you.

Language:

It is often said that French people do not speak English and do not like trying. French pupils learn English at school for six years, so every French person (particularly the younger generation) has at least a basic knowledge of the English language and is able to understand. They might, however, not always feel comfortable speaking English.

Staff in hotels, restaurants and popular tourist destinations and monuments however always speak English and all brochures, maps, documentation etc. are available in a wide variety of languages. You are most welcome to speak French if you can, it will be appreciated.

Public Toilets:

These are a challenge in Paris. Various types of automatic self-standing public toilets are available on the pavements in Paris, but may not always work or a may be a bit intimidating to use. After each person uses the toilet, the door will close and the toilet will "clean" itself. These are free to use but are usually not very clean in reality. If you do not let the toilet clean itself, the door will not close.

Public toilets in Métro stations, monuments or museums are not always free. There is usually an attendant, and you may choose to leave a few coins in the saucer provided, as a tip, if you wish.

Appliances:

France uses a 220V electricity system and 2 pin plugs. Make sure that your hairdryer, chargers etc... are compatible, or buy an adaptor before leaving your home country or at the airport on arrival, as these adaptors are not readily available inside Paris. Some devices will need more than just an adapter and will need a pricier power/voltage converter, otherwise they may malfunction or explode. Be sure to check your devices and chargers to see what voltage they support, and make sure that 220V is included in this range. Most modern smartphones for example will charge in the 110V-240V spectrum, meaning they will work fine in France.

Smoking in France:

Smoking is not allowed in public places in France. Some restaurants still allow smoking on the terrace. There are no smoking sections in restaurants. Be aware, though, that smoking in France is very widespread and it is still a national trait. You will certainly encounter your fair share of cigarette smoke while moving through the city.

Transport – Getting to Paris

By Air

Paris is easily accessible with all major domestic and international airlines through its three airports:

Aéroport Roissy Charles de Gaulle (CDG)

Situated 32kms north of Paris, Roissy Charles de Gaulle is Europe's busiest airport. It deals with the majority of international long distance flights. A wide variety of transport options are available for travellers to reach the centre of Paris.

Contact information:
Telephone: +33 (0)1 70 36 39 50
Website: www.aeroportsdeparis.fr
Free WiFi is available throughout the airport

CDG Public Transport:
RER B - This train line runs between central Paris and the airport. From Terminals 1, 2 & 3 to *Gare du Nord, Chatelet les Halles, Notre Dame, Denfert Rochereau*. Cost: €9.75 / Transit time: 25 to 35 minutes
Bus 350 - To Gare de l'Est. Cost: €6 / Transit time: 80 minutes
Bus 351 - To Nation. Cost:€6 / Transit time: 80 to 90 minutes
Roissybus - To Opéra. Cost: €11 / Transit time: 60 minutes
Les Cars Air France 3 – To Orly airport. Cost: €17.50 / Transit time: 1h15
Les Cars Air France 4 – To Gare de Lyon and Gare Montparnasse - Cost: €21/ Transit time: 1h15
Prices are subject to change. Approximate average transit times given. Can be increased or decreased according to traffic conditions.

CDG Taxis:
A large variety of taxis are available outside the terminals in designated areas.
Rates: Taxis charge per kilometre and per minute (to allow for waiting time or heavy traffic). Luggage is charged per item, usually the first item is included in the price. The following are average prices and transfer times.
* Roissy Charles de Gaulle to Champs Elysées +/- €55* – 34 minutes
* Roissy Charles de Gaulle to Chatelet les Halles +/- €48* – 36 minutes
* Roissy Charles de Gaulle to Notre Dame de Paris +/- €51* – 42 minutes

CDG Shuttle Services:

Many private shuttle services ("navettes") are available linking Roissy Charles de Gaulle and central Paris. A choice of private or shared shuttle services is available. These must be booked in advance. A direct shuttle service to Disneyland Paris is also available and priced at €20 per person with a journey time of 45 minutes. Available at www.magicalshuttle.co.uk.

Trusted shuttle companies includes: **Super Shuttle Paris** - www.supershuttle.com; **Club Shuttle** - www.clubshuttle.fr; **Paris City Vision** - www.pariscityvision.com; and **Paris Navettes** - www.paris-navettes.fr.

CDG Car Hire:

All major international and local car hire companies are present at the airport, and have desks at all terminals. Hire companies include: Advantage, Alamo, Avis, Budget, Dollar, Enterprise, Europcar, Firefly, Hertz, Interrent, National, Sixt, Thrifty and TT Transit.

Aéroport d'Orly (ORY)

Situated 20km south of Paris and France's 2nd busiest airport, Aéroport d'Orly accommodates short haul flights mostly to and from Europe.

Contact information:

Telephone: +33 (0)1 70 36 39 50
Website: www.aeroportsdeparis.fr
Free WiFi is available throughout the airport

Orly Public Transport:

- **Tramway and Métro line 7** – To Métro Villejuif Aragon
- **Bus 183** – To Porte de Choisy
- **Bus 91-10** – To Gare de Massy-TGV
- **Orlybus** – To Denfert Rochereau
- **Les Cars Air France 3** – To Roissy Charles de Gaulle
- **OrlyVal** – To Antony

Orly Taxis:

A large variety of taxis are available outside the terminals in designated areas.

Orly Shuttle Services:
Shuttle services are available to and from Orly including **Les Cars Airfrance** from *Place d'Etoile, Les Invalides, Gare Montparnasse* or *Gare de Lyon* to Orly airport. Transfer times are 45 minutes to 1 hour depending on where you get on and off. Tickets cost €12.50 one-way or €21 round trip.

For those travelling direct to Disneyland Paris, there is the **Magical Shuttle Disneyland Paris** service. Book at www.magicalshuttle.co.uk.

Orly Car Hire:
All major international and local car hire companies are present at the airport, and have desks at all terminals. Hire companies include: Avis, Advantage, Europcar, National Citer, Hertz, Sixt and TT Transit.

Aéroport de Paris Beauvais-Tillé

The name of this airport is a quite misleading in our opinion, as it is in fact not located anywhere near Paris. It is 75km north of the city. This is the low-cost airport of choice for Paris. Be aware that transfer times are long to and from the city.

Contact information:
Telephone: +33 892 68 20 66
Website: www.aeroportbeauvais.com

Beauvais Transfer options:
- A Shuttle (Navette) operating from *Paris Porte Maillot* to *Aéroport de Beauvais* is available (1h 15m transfer time) - €17 one-way
- A taxi will cost about €100 to €160 one way from the airport to Paris
- Car hire desks at the airport include Avis, Budget, Europcar, Hertz, Enterprise and Sixt.

By Rail:

The seven major railway stations across Paris each serve a specific region or destination. Wherever you are in France, rest assured that you will be able to reach Paris easily and rapidly by rail. The national railway company, SNCF, operates the rail system. High-speed TGV trains *(Train à Grande Vitesse)*, as well as conventional slower commuter services operate out of all these stations. Some stations also offer international train services.

- **Gare d'Austerlitz** *(7bis Boulevard de l'Hôpital, 75013 Paris)* – Trains to and from Orléans and the south of France
- **Gare du Nord** *(112 Rue de Maubeuge, 75010 Paris)* – Trains to and from the north of France, including the Thalys system (Brussels, Liège, Amsterdam), and the Eurostar to and from London.
- **Gare de l'Est** *(Place du 11 novembre 1918, 75011 Paris)* – Trains to and from the east of France, as well as international lines such as Frankfurt, Berlin and Zurich. Home to TGV Est to Strasbourg.
- **Gare de Lyon** *(Place Louis Armand, 75012 Paris)* – Trains to and from the south and east of France and Europe.
- **Gare Saint Lazare** *(13 Rue d'Amsterdam, 75008 Paris)* – Trains to and from suburbs and Normandy.
- **Gare Montparnasse** *(Place Raoul Dautry, 75015 Paris)* – Trains to and from west of France: Brittany, Tours, Bordeaux.
- **Gare de Paris-Bercy** *(48 bis Boulevard de Bercy, 75012 Paris)* – Used by the AutoTrain srevice that carries cars onboard to the south of France.

TGV trains are the best way to get across large distances quickly in France. Trains reach 320km/h (200mph), making them much quicker than driving. The trains must be booked in advance. This can be done either at a station before travelling (though, not that limited seats are available), at a kiosk or online. We recommend booking TGV trains in advance online at www.voyages-sncf.com where timetables can easily be checked.

By Road:

France is extremely well equipped with a vast structured network of highways as well as national, regional and departmental roads, ensuring that even the most remote of villages are easily accessible.

Highways (motorways) are usually toll roads, but are the fastest route between major cities. One can however decide to take National or Regional roads and admire the scenery of the French countryside and reach Paris a little later but having had a different experience, as well as avoiding the toll fees.

Paris is surrounded by the "périphérique", a ring road on the perimeter of the city, with entrances and exits located at strategic points. When enquiring about an address that you wish to reach by road, ask for directions including the nearest périphéque exit.

Transport – Getting around Paris
Métro and RER

From humble beginnings in 1900, the Métro de Paris has grown into a modern transport network, not only connecting the various areas of the city, but also the suburbs. With 16 interconnecting underground lines and 5 wider-reaching RER lines, the network is the most popular and practical way to travel around Paris.

Paris' metro lines are underground subway lines that cover the centre of the city, whereas the RER lines *(Réseau Express Régional / 'Regional Express Network')* start in the centre and go well into the suburbs in almost every direction. The RERs run at higher speeds and are useful for travelling long distances – think of it as a high-speed, long-distance metro network.

Transfers between the two systems are done within large, mostly underground, stations. The fare system is integrated between the two, and you should largely think of the system is being one. Just make sure your ticket covers the zones you need to travel in.

Note that neither the metro, nor the RER system offer 24-hour transport solutions, though they do run fairly late and start fairly early (times vary by station and line). In the early hours of the morning, night buses are your only public transport option. General operating hours for the metro are 5:30am to 1:15am on Monday to Thursday and Sundays. On Friday and Saturday nights the metro will closes one hour later, at around 2:15am. RER services vary but they generally run from 5:30am to midnight daily.

If you need to plan a journey be sure to run an itinerary through the RATP website at **http://www.ratp.info/orienter/itineraire.php**. This is particularly useful for finding the first and last trains of the day on a particular route.

Step by Step – using the Metro and RER:
The start – You will begin your journey by going to the ticket barrier. Here you will either: 1) need to insert a paper travel ticket into and then take it back before the automatic doors open, or 2) scan your electronic smartcard on a reader that allows you through the doors. Option 2 is usually reserved to Parisians with regular travel cards.

Selecting your platform – Once through the ticket barriers, you will need to follow the signs to the metro or RER line you wish to use, going in the correct direction. Be 100% sure of the direction of travel. At some stations there are separate ticket barriers for each direction, so be sure to know where you are going before you put your ticket through the barrier. Be aware that if you end up going in the wrong direction, this could cost you not only time, but the price of a second ticket to go to back in the direction you originally intended to go.

Confirm your destination – Once on the platform you will want to be sure that your train will serve the station you are travelling to. Metro trains stop at all the stations on a particular line. RER trains, however, stop at all stations in central Paris but only stop at selected stations outside of central Paris. Be sure to checked the departure screens for the list of stations your RER train will call at.

Boarding the train – At the vast majority of lines once the train stops on the platforms, the doors will not open automatically – each door is opened manually. You will need to either press a button, or lift a lever to open the doors. On some lines all doors open automatically. Make sure to allow people off the train first before boarding yourself *(unfortunately many people in Paris do not follow this rule, unlike in London)*. Mind the gap between the train and the platform at many stations.

On the train – Take a seat if there are any available, and pay attention to the stops. There may be verbal and visual announcements, or nothing at all (in which case your transport map will come in handy) depending on the line you are on.

Getting off – Be up and ready to leave to train before it stops at your station. The doors will either need to be open manually, or they will be automatic as mentioned before.

Transfers – If transferring lines between the metro and RER, you may need to re-scan your ticket through the ticket barrier during transfers.

Exiting – Depending on where you exit you will either need to insert your paper ticket to go through a ticket barrier, or you will just walk out through a large one-way door without needing to insert your ticket.

Buses and Trams

The first public transport system first appeared in Paris in 1828, when regular Omnibus lines started successfully. The bus transport system now boasts a total of 200 lines over the entire Parisian region (around 60 in the city centre), and thousands of bus stops that are strategically positioned to ensure that every corner of Paris is covered. Buses generally run from 5:30am to midnight every day. The frequency of services depends on the time of day and the day of the week.

A large variety of tickets are available, from the single trip ticket (Ticket T+) to passes valid for unlimited travel over several days. Tickets and passes are available at the various stations as well as online at **www.ratp.fr** and **www.parisinfo.com**.

Many bus stops provide live bus arrival screens in order to facilitate your journey. Neighbourhood maps and transfer maps are usually displayed at each bus stop, as are first and last bus times.

Note that buses will be busy during peak hours. Remember to check first and last bus times as these vary depending on the bus route you are taking.

Passengers board the bus via the front door. Tickets must be validated when boarding (for single-journey paper tickets this means inserting them into a machine near the driver) – ask for *"la machine à composter".* Do not validate *Paris Visite* tickets on the buses, simply show these to the driver.

Nightbus lines *(Noctiliens)* provide nighttime services when normal bus routes do not run. Noctilien buses generally run from 00:30 to 05:30.

Rates: The rates vary from €1.80 for a single trip ticket, to €67 for a 5-day adult pass. Note that single trip tickets do not allow transfers if your ticket is bought on the bus. The pre-paid Ticket T+ allows transfers for 90 minutes (see ticketing section). Be sure to have exact change if purchasing tickets on the bus.

Paris currently has 8 tramlines, although these are unlikely to be used by visitors. They function very similarly to buses in terms of operation, and standard metro and bus tickets and fares apply.

Balabus – This is a bus rotue designed for visitors which connects many of central Paris' sites. Stops include La Defense, the Arc de Triomphe, Champs Elysées, the Louvre, Notre Dame, Gare de Lyon, Opéra, Notre Dame, Musée d'Orsay, les Invalides and the Eiffel Tower, to name but a few. This is an impressive line up and at first hand it seems like the perfect travel solution.

However, unfortunately, we are not sure why Paris even bothers providing this service - its usefulness is limited as it only runs from April to September, on Sundays and public holidays in the afternoon between 12:30 and 20:00. You can use only Ticket T+s or the Paris Visite passes on these buses. the front of buses displays 'Bb' instead of the bus number.

Public Transport Tickets

A large variety of tickets are available, from the single trip ticket to passes valid for unlimited travel over several days. Tickets and passes are available to purchase at all metro and RER stations from ticket counters and automated machines (which accept cash and cards), as well as online at **www.ratp.fr** and **www.parisinfo.com.** We recommend you purchase your ticket at the station.

Ticket T+

The small *Ticket T+* tickets are the most widely-used tickets by visitors and are great value for money. Once bought these tickets do not expire and if you have any leftover tickets you can bring these back during your next trip to Paris.

The *Ticket T+* is single-fare ticket that allows unlimited travel on the whole of the metro system, on buses and trams, and on zone 1 RER (Regional trains).

The cost is just €1.80 per trip per ticket. A discount of 27% is available for purchasing 10 tickets *(un carnet)* at a time – 10 tickets cost €14,10. A carnet is ten individual tickets, meaning that a group of five could each travel twice with these tickets. Children under 10 years old can get a 50% discount. You can use the Ticket T+ over the course of your trip as and when you need, as they do not expire.

You can change (transfer) between metro lines and the RER an unlimited number of times within 90 minutes from when the ticket was first validated. You can also change between bus routes, and between buses and trams during 90 minutes from first validation too. You cannot use a single Ticket T+ to ride the metro, followed by a bus or tram (or vice-versa) – in this case you will need two separate tickets.

34

Top Tip: You should make sure to buy your Ticket T+ from a metro station for the most flexibility. This is because tickets bought on board buses cost €2 each instead of €1.80 and crucially do *not* allow transfers (meaning you will need to buy a separate ticket for each bus you board). You cannot buy *un carnet* on board a bus.

Billet Origine-Destination (rail only):

If you will be travelling outside the two central zones on the metro, or outside zone 1 on the RER you will need an *Origine-Destination* ticket. You can buy these tickets at a machine or from a member of staff. Your starting station will be where you currently are, and you will select your destination. You can then use the tickets to travel between the two locations, in either direction. Prices vary depending on the distance travelled.

Tickets with a destination or a starting point in central Paris allow you to enter and exit anywhere in central Paris, using the metro and RER (zone 1 only) as a method of transfer.

Mobilis:

This is a day pass option that allows you unlimited travel for the day between the zones of your choosing. You can use all forms of transport within Paris including Métro, RER, Bus, Transilien trains and Trams. However, your tickets will not allow you to access *Charles de Gaulle* airport or *Orly* airport stations. For access to the airports you will need either a single "*Origine-Destination*" ticket or a Paris Visite ticket. Mobilis pricing is as follows:

- Zones 1 to 2 - €7,00
- Zones 1 to 3 - €9,30
- Zones 1 to 4 - €11,50
- Zones 1 to 5 - €16,60

Half price child rates are available. Make sure to write the day of use on the front of your ticket.

Paris Visite:

This is another day pass option which may make more sense to some visitors. It allows you unlimited travel and you can choose the zones, as well as how many days the ticket lasts for. You can use all forms of transport within Paris including Métro, RER, Bus, Trams, Transilien trains, the OrlyVal and the Monmartre funicular railway. If you get the zones 1 to 5 ticket, you can also travel to and from CDG and Orly airports.

The pass also offers discounts from 13 partners include 20% off entry to the Arc de Triomphe, 30% off entry to Tour Montparnasse and €10 off each Disneyland Paris ticket. If you are planning on using public transport regularly for your Parisian trip, this ticket can very quickly pay for itself.

Paris Visite ticket prices for zones 1 to 3 are as follows:
  - 1 day - €12,30
  - 2 days - €20,00
  - 3 days - €27,30
  - 5 days - €39,30

Paris Visite ticket prices for zones 1 to 5 are as follows:
  - 1 day - €25,85
  - 2 days - €39,30
  - 3 days - €55,10
  - 5 days - €67,40

Children under 10 get a 50% discount off these prices.

Bicycle – Vélib

Paris has been home to the bike rental system, Velib, since 2009. It is a fun and eco-friendly way to visit the city, and the system is completely self-service. Casual users do not even need to register in advance.

Simply show up at any of the Velib docking stations and follow the terminal's on-screen instructions, you will need to pay for your bike rental with a payment card, and then you will simply collect one of the bikes. There are over 1800 stations which are easily recognisable, with one every 300 metres.

You can put your bike back at any Velib station around the city provided there are free spaces. Simply push your bike all the way into the docking point return it. If you turn up to a station and find no free spaces, simply use the docking terminal to get an addition 15 minutes to return your bike to another station.

Rates: There are two kinds of pricing systems in place at the same time. You must first pay to access the system, and then you must pay a usage fee depending on how long you use the system for. A 1-day access pass is priced at €1.70. A 7-day pass is only €8. Various pass options are available for longer time periods. Each journey under 30 minutes in length is free, and the usage fee is then €1 per every 30 minutes thereafter. You can make an unlimited number of journeys lasting under 30 minute throughout the day and only pay the daily charge. 30 minute is usually more than enough for most journeys. You can enquire, book and learn more online at **www.velib.paris.fr**.

Autolib

Autolib is essentially 'Velib' (see above) but for cars. It does, however, require more of a time commitment to get started than Velib. This is an all-electric car-sharing scheme where you can get a car from one of the various parking spaces, drive it, and then return it to any other free autolib parking space.

To use the system register at autolib.eu (and wait for your usage card in the post), at the on-street subscription kiosks at certain Autolib locations (small rooms on the street where you will video call with an operator who will guide you through the process and deliver you usage card instantly) or at the Autolib centre located at 5, rue Edouard VII, Paris in the 9th arrondissement. You will need your driving license (only International and European driving licenses are accepted), a valid ID (passport or national identity card) and a credit card (Visa or Mastercard) to register.

Once registered you can make reservations online, or via the Autolib smartphone apps. Then, go to your pickup location. Here you will need to scan your usage card (that you obtained during registration) on the charge point, you will then unlock the car by scanning your card over blue light by the driver's window. Make sure that the charging cable is put back correctly in its charging point.

After driving around town and running your errands, you can park your car at any empty autolib parking space (identifiable with a green light on the charge point). Here you will scan your card on the charge point, connect the electric charging cable to the car, and lock your car by scanning your card by the driver's window.

Rates: Like Velib, there is a charge to access the system, and then a charge for the time you use. For a one-day access there is no system access charge, and each minute of driving costs €0.30. 7-day access to the system costs €10, plus €0.23 per minute. A 1-month access pass costs €25, plus €0.21 per minute driven. There is a minimum charge of 20 minutes of driving per rental. There are no insurance, fuel or maintenance charges with this system.

On foot

One of the best ways to explore Paris and experience the atmosphere, the vibe and the history of this great city is to walk. Whether you are interested in history and architecture, the typical Parisian atmosphere, a tour of restaurants or a shopping spree, walking around is the best way to experience this beautiful location.

Due to the city's major rebuilding between the 1850s and 1870s, the city boasts large pavements (sidewalks) and many parks, making it one of the best cities in the world to explore on foot. Paris' current mayor is currently on a battle to pedestrianize a lot of areas of the city in order to make the city even more friendly to those who like to walk around.

Taxis

Taxis can be an efficient way for large groups to get across Paris, particularly if you do not want to learn the ins and outs of the public transportation system, or have heavy suitcases or shopping to carry. The word "cab" is not widely used or recognised in France, and taxi is preferable.

Parisian taxis are expensive and public transport can be both quicker and cheaper, depending on the journey. However, it is the sheer convenience of taxi services that make them so popular.

Taxis in Paris are difficult to hail and instead you should look out for one of the city's taxi ranks *(une station de taxi)*, this is because there are a multitude of rules including that taxis may not pick you up if you are within 50m of a taxi rank. If there is no taxi rank nearby you should be able to hail a cab fairly easily. A green light on the top of a taxi means it is available, red means it is not.

There are over 700 taxi ranks in the central Paris zone alone. Taxi ranks are identified by a blue square with white writing on it saying "TAXIS". There will either be a taxi waiting, or you can hail a taxi easily. Some will also provide a telephone to call for a taxi.

Rates: Pricing for taxis can be expensive. Be sure that the taxi you are using has a meter – this is extremely important. The starting price for a standard car journey is €2.60, with a minimum fare of €7. The price per kilometre is between €1.05 and €1.56, and the per minute rate varies between €1.06 and €1.20. If taxis are driving slowly or are stopped, the minute rate applies; otherwise you will be billed per kilometre. Your total fare will be a combination of both these charges.

As an example, a 15-minute sample journey (such as the Eiffel Tower to the Louvre) should cost between €11 and €13 in inner Paris, and €14 to €19 in greater Paris.

Then there are the "hidden charges". If there are more than 3 passengers travelling there is a €3 surcharge, and it is €1 per piece of luggage after the first. Finally, there is the waiting time charge – this can be high if you are specifically calling a taxi for yourself. The driver is allowed to switch on the meter from the moment he leaves to meet you, not from when he actually arrives at your destination – this means that it is common for more than the minimum fare to be displayed on the meter when your taxi arrives.

If you prefer to pre-book, two well-know companies that operate in Paris are "Taxis G7" (01 41 27 66 99) and "Central Taxi Parisien" (call 01 47 46 91 52). Operators generally speak English, or can transfer you to someone else who can.

Some taxi companies allow you to book via smartphone apps. Search "Paris Taxi" on your smartphone's app store. Remember you will need an internet connection for this.

Finally, Uber (a worldwide on-demand ride service) is another option for users, with prices generally being 50% or less than regular taxi prices. Reservations are made through the Uber app. As an example, a 15-minute sample journey (eg. Tour Eiffel to the Louvre) should cost between €6 and €8 with UberPop, or €10 to €13 with UberX. The legality of Uber is currently in question in the country, and the service is very controversial.

Use our special link at **www.uber.com/invite/uberindependentguides** to receive $20/€10/£10 free credit, meaning your first ride could be at no cost to you.

Paris Attractions: District by District

Here we a look at Paris' attractions, these are split by arrondissement (district) to make the city easy to navigate. You can get between the attractions in an arrondissement easily on foot. This section focuses on the attractions; with separate sections for dining and accommodation.

1st Arrondissement: Le Louvre

The first arrondissement is one of the oldest with the *île de la cité* section dating back to 52 BC. Less than 20,000 people live in this area making it the least populated. The area is largely devoted to museums and attractions.

Musée de L'Orangerie

Address: Jardin des Tuileries , 75001 Paris
Telephone: 01 44 50 43 00
Website: www.musee-orangerie.fr
Open: Six days a week from 9:00am to 6:00pm. Closed every Tuesday, 1st May, 14th July and 25th December.
Rates: Access to Orsay and Orangerie Museums - €16 / Adults - €9 / Reduced rate - €6.50.
Access: Métro Lines 1, 8 and 12 *Concorde* / Bus Routes 24, 42, 52, 72, 73, 83, 84 and 94, Balabus *Cité* stop

Located in a building dating back to 1852, the *Musée de l'Orangerie* was Claude Monet's choice for his famous masterpiece Les Nympheas, that covers one half of the wall space. The rest of the museum is dedicated to the permanent collection, as well as temporary special exhibitions.

Palais de la Cité / Conciergerie

Address: 2 Boulevard du Palais, 75001 Paris
Telephone: 01 53 40 60 80
Website: http://conciergerie.monuments-nationaux.fr/
Open: Every day from 9:30am to 6:00pm (last entry 5:30pm). Closed on 1st January, 1st May and 25th December
Rates: Adult over 26 - € 8.50/ Ages 18-25 - € 5.50 / Under 18 – Free / Disabled Person and helper - Free
Access: Métro Lines 1, 4, 7, 11 & 14 *Cité* station / RER Lines B & C *Saint Michel-Notre Dame* station / Bus Routes 21, 24, 27, 38, 58, 81 and 85, Balabus *Cité* stop

Home to the French government between the 10th and 14th centuries, the *Palais de la Cité* (also known as the *Conciergerie*) was converted into a prison in 1370. This is where royal Marie Antoinette was held in 1793, before being beheaded during the French revolution. Today, most of the premises is used by the Paris Tribunal, with the historical parts that remain being the prison and the Chapel (*Sainte-Chapelle*).

Palais Royal

Address: 8 Rue Montpensier, 75001 Paris
Telephone: 01 47 03 92 16
Website: http://palais-royal.monuments-nationaux.fr.
Open: Daily. Garden and courtyard open at 7:00am and close at 8:30pm in winter and 11:30pm in summer. Gallery opening hours vary.
Rates: Free
Access: Métro Lines 1, 7 and 14 *Palais Royal* / Bus Routes 21, 27, 39, 48, 69, 72, 81 and 95, Balabus *Cité* stop

Built in 1628 by Richelieu, the *Palais Royal* was residence to several kings. An impressive, building surrounding luxurious gardens, it is also a theatre hall, home of the famous French theatre company *La Comédie Française* since 1799.

Jardin des Tuileries

Address: 113 Rue de Rivoli, 75001 Paris
Website: www.gardenvisit.com/garden/jardin_des_tuileries
Open: Daily from 11:00am to 7:00pm
Rates: Free
Access: Métro Line 1 *Tuileries* / Bus Routes 21, 24, 27, 39, 48, 68, 69, 72, 81, 95, Balabus *Cité* stop

Surrounded by the *Palais du Louvre*, *Place de la Concorde* and the *Seine* River, this is the oldest landscaped garden in Paris. Magnificent, peaceful and a pleasure to walk in, this site is registered as a World Heritage site by UNESCO.

Musée du Louvre

Address: Musee du Louvre, 75001 Paris
Telephone: 01 40 20 53 17
Website: www.louvre.fr/en
Open: Six days a week. Closed on Tuesdays. Also closed on 1ˢᵗ May, 14ᵗʰ July and 25ᵗʰ December. Open from 9:00am to 6:00pm on Monday, Thursday, Saturday and Sunday. Open from 9:00am to 9:45pm on Wednesdays and Fridays.
Rates: Access to Le Louvre & Eugene Delacroix Museums - €12 / Access to Napoleon Hall - €13 / Full Access - €16 / Free access everyone aged under 18, and for European residents between the age of 18 and 25.
Access: Métro Line 1, 7 *Palais Royal Le Louvre* /Bus Routes 21, 24, 27, 39, 48, 68, 69, 72, 81 and 95, Balabus *Cité* stop.

An art and antiques museum, this is one of the largest museums in the world and home to the famous Mona Lisa *(La Joconde)*, as well as an impressive collection of other masterpieces. The glass pyramid erected in 1983 is now the entrance to the museum, and adds a touch of modernism to the site.

Top Tip: The 'main' entrance to the museum via the Pyramid has exceptionally long security queue lines year-round. However, the entrance via the *Carrousel du Louvre* shopping centre has much shorter, and faster-moving, queues year-round. To get there, look for the *Arc de Triomphe du Carrousel* which is the archway visible on the other side of the roundabout nearby. On each side of the archway there is a staircase which leads down to the shopping centre. There is another entrance to the shopping centre on Rue de Rivoli with the shopping centre name written, you will take an escalator downstairs. Inside this shopping centre is another entrance to the museum.

Ile de la Cité

Address: Ile de la Cité, 75001 Paris
Open: Public area, open all the time
Rates: Free
Access: Metro Line 4 *Cité*, RER Lines B and C *Saint-Michel – Notre Dame*

The *Ile de la Cité* is Paris' historical center where the medieval city was re-established. It was a political and military centre with natural defense against invasion - water. The *Ile de la Cité* is home to numerous famous Parisian monuments such as the *Cathedrale Notre Dame*, the *Palais de Justice* and *la Sainte-Chapelle*, the *Conciergerie*, the *Place Dauphine*, and the *Pont Neuf* (the oldest bridge in Paris). The *Ile de la Cité* remains the heart of Paris and all road distances in France are calculated from the *Place du Parvis de Notre Dame* here, where you will find a commemorative plaque.

La Sainte Chapelle

Address: 8, Bouleveard du Palais, 75001 Paris
Telephone: 01 53 40 60 80
Website: http://sainte-chapelle.monuments-nationaux.fr/
Open: 7 days a week from 9:30am to 5:00pm in winter, and 6:00pm in summer.
Rates: Standard tariff: €8.50. Free for anyone under 18 and for europeen residents under 25.
Access: Métro Lines 1 & 11 & 14 *Hotel de Ville- Chatelet* and Line 4 *Saint Michel* and Line 7 *Chatelet* and Line 10 *Sorbonne* / RER Line B & C *Saint Michel - Notre Dame* / Bus Routes 21, 24, 27, 36, 38, 47, 85 and 96

The *Sainte-Chapelle* is situated near the *Cathedrale Notre Dame*, and was built in the 12th century. It is a jewel of Gothic art classed by UNESCO. The upper chapel is covered by 600 square metres of stained glass window of which two thirds are still originals. *La Sainte-Chapelle*, with the *Conciergerie*, is one of the earliest surviving of the capetian royal palace on the *Ile de la cité*. The Sainte Chapelle has just come out of refurbishment in Spring 2015 and is well worth a visit.

2nd and 3rd Arrondissements: La Bourse and Le Temple

The second arrondissement, *La Bourse*, is home to the *Place de la Bourse* where a food market takes place from noon to 8:00pm on Tuesdays and Fridays. There are also historic stock exchange buildings here, and the previous home of the national French library. Today, *La Bourse* is home to 20,000 residents.

Le Temple is today home to a couple of notable museums, as well as *51 Rue de Montmorency* – the oldest house in Paris, made from stone and built in 1407. The famous and fashionable *Le Marais* district is spread across this arrondissement and the 4th.

Musée Carnavalet

Address: 16 Rue des Francs Bourgeois, 75003 Paris
Telephone: 01 44 59 58 58
Website: www.carnavalet.paris.fr/en
Open: Tuesday to Sunday from 10:00am to 6:00pm. Closed every Monday and 1st May
Rates: The permanent collection is free. Fees for temporary exhibitions, lectures and cultural activities/workshops vary, but are free for under 18s.
Access: Métro Line 1 *Saint Paul* and Line 8 *Chemin Vert* / Bus Lines 29, 69, 76 and 96

Dedicated to the history of Paris and its inhabitants, art collections depict the evolution of Paris from the prehistoric era to today through paintings, objects, models, sculptures and various artworks. A very good way to understand the Paris of today.

Musée Picasso

Address: 5 Rue de Thorigny, 75003 Paris
Telephone: 01 85 56 00 36
Website: www.museepicassoparis.fr/en
Open: Tuesday to Sunday from 10:00am to 6:00pm, with the museum opening 30 minutes earlier on the weekend. Closed every Monday and on 1st January, 1st May and 25th December.
Rates: Full tariff - €11 / €15 with multimedia guide / Free for under 18s and for Europeen citizen under 26 / Free access for all on the 1st Sunday of each month.
Access: Métro Line 1 *Saint Paul* and Line 8 *Chemin Vert* or *Saint Sebastien Froissard* / Bus Lines 20, 29, 65, 69, 75 and 96

Learn all about Pablo Picasso from his life to his work through personal documents and archives, as well as his personal collection of classic paintings. Various punctual events and special exhibitions are organised regularly.

4th Arrondissement: L'Hôtel de Ville

This arrondissement is home to some of the city's most beautiful monuments. It also encompasses the marvelous *Ile Saint Louis*. Furthermore, the 4th is home to *Le Marais*, a fashionable area which spans the 4th and 3rd arrondissements.

Ile Saint Louis

Address: Ile Saint Louis, 75001 Paris
Open: Public area, open all the time
Rates: Free
Access: Métro Line *4 Saint Paul* and Line 7 *Pont Marie* and Line 10 *Cardinal Lemoine* / Bus Lines: 24, 67, 86 and 87

The *Ile Saint Louis* is the second natural island on the *Seine* river. The island was primarily used as a market for cattle, and for stocking wood. Designed and built during the 17th century under Henry IV and Louis XII, the island is a peaceful oasis in the centre of Paris with narrow one-way streets. Today, it is a famous residential area with several restaurants, hotels, shops and cafés. The island is connected to Paris by 4 bridges and to *Ile de la Cité* by the small *Pont Saint Louis* where one can enjoy live performers (Jazz bands, mimes, singers, clowns…). Don't forget to visit the *Eglise Saint Louis,* a stunning church.

Hotel de Ville

Address: Place de L'hotel de Ville, 75004 Paris
Telephone: 01 42 76 43 43
Website: http://en.parisinfo.com/musee-monument-paris/71544/H%C3%B4tel-de-Ville-de-Paris
Open: Twice a week during the summer (closed on weekends) and by appointment only – this must be made a minimum of 1 week before your visit
Rates: Free
Access: Métro Lines 1, 11 *Hotel de Ville* / RER Line B *Chatelet les Halles* / Bus Lines 38, 47, 67, 69, 70, 72, 74, 75,76, 85 and 96, Balabus *Cité* stop

Since 1357, Paris' municipal offices and institutions have been in the same location. Now called Hotel de Ville, this majestuous building is beautifully decorated and home to a number of official events. The *Salle des Fêtes* in particular is an architectural gem, a replica of the *Galerie des Glaces* (hall of mirrors) in Versailles.

Musée Centre Georges Pompidou

Address: Place Georges Pompidou, 75004 Paris
Telephone: 01 44 78 12 33
Website: www.centrepompidou.fr/en/The-Centre-Pompidou
Open: Six days a week from 11:00am to 10:00pm. Closed Tuesday, and 1st May
Rates: Full Tariff: €14 / Free for under 18s
Access: Métro Line 1 *Rambuteau*, Lines 1 and 4 *Hotel de Ville*, Lines 1, 4, 7, 11 and 14 *Chatelet les Halles* / RER A and B *Chatelet les Halles* / Bus Lines 24, 38, 47 and 75

Known for its very specific and futuristic architecture, the Centre Pompidou has been a high point of the Parisian cultural life since 1977. Art gallery regrouping paintings as well as other forms of visual arts, a mediatheque and a public library, a visit will bring you an experience well beyond one of a standard museum.

Place des Vosges Square Louis XIII

Address: 30 Place des Vosges, 75004 Paris
Website: http://equipement.paris.fr/square-louis-xiii-36
Open: 365 days a year. From May to August Monday to Friday: 08.30 am to 9.30 pm. On Saturday and Sunday: 09.00 am to 9.30 pm. Hours are shorter throughout the rest of the year, determined by the time of sunset.
Rates: Free
Access: Métro Line 1 *Saint Paul* and Line 5 *Bastille* and Line 8 *Chemin Vert* / Bus Lines 20, 29, 65 and 96

Located in the Marais district, Square Louis XIII is situated in the centre of the sumptuous *Place des Vosges*. This park is the oldest park in the city and was built by Henry IV and inaugurated in 1612 for Louis XII's wedding. This park, lined with trees and the famous redbrick house with blue roof, is home to large lawns with a fountain in the centre, as well as an equestrian statue of Louis the XIII himself.

Cathedrale Notre-Dame de Paris

Address: 6 Parvis Notre Dame/Place Jean Paul II, 75004 Paris
Website: www.notredamedeparis.fr
Open: Daily from 8.00am to 6:45pm (and 7:15pm on Saturday and Sunday)
Rates: Free
Access: Métro: Lines 1 & 11 & 14 *Hotel de Ville - Chatelet*, Line 4 *Saint Michel*, Line 7 *Chatelet* and Line 10 *Sorbonne* / RER: Line B & C *Saint Michel - Notre Dame* / Bus Lines: 21, 24, 27, 36, 38, 47, 85 and 96

Notre Dame is the most visited monument in France, with upwards of 14 million visitors a year. It is a masterpiece of French Gothic architecture. Its construction began in the XIII century and finished only in the XV century. Its vast interior accommodates 6000 worshipers. Highlights include its three spectacular rose windows, the treasury, and the bell towers which can be climbed, 400 steps spiral to the top where you will find yourself face to face with frightening gargoyles and a spectacular view over Paris.

5th Arrondissement: Le Panthéon

The *Panthéon* arrondissement is notable for being home to the Latin Quarter which is filled with prestigous educational institutions. It is also one of the city's oldest areas.

The Panthéon

Address: Place du Panthéon, 75005 Paris
Telephone: 01 44 32 18 00
Website: http://pantheon.monuments-nationaux.fr/
Open: Every day from 10:00am to 8:00pm (last entry at 7:00pm). Closed on 1st May.
Rates: Adult over 26 - € 10 / Ages 18 to 25 - € 8 / Under 18s go free
Access: RER Line B *Denfert Rochereau* station / Bus 68 *Denfert Rochereau* stop

In the centre of the *Place Panthéon*, originally destined to be a church in the 18th century, the *Panthéon* honours the great people who played a role in France's history. Great writers, poets, artists, politicians and war heroes are buried here. From the architecture to the beautiful views from the dome, the *Panthéon* is must-see in Paris.

Musée de Cluny

Address: 6, Place Paul Painleve, 75005 Paris
Telephone: 01 53 73 78 00/16
Website: www.musee-moyenage.fr
Open: 6 days a week from 9:15am to 5:45pm. Closed Tuesdays and 1st January, 1st May and 25th December.
Rates: Full tariff - €9 / Reduced tariff - €7 / Free for chidren under 18 and for EU residents under 26 / Free for all the first Sunday of each month.
Access: Métro Lines 4 *Saint Michel Odeon*, Line 10 *Cluny - La Sorbonne* / RER Line B and C *Saint Michel - Notre Dame* / Bus Routes 21, 27, 38, 63, 85, 86 and 87

This museum focuses on the medieval ages, and covers everything from the culture, to the science, and even the art of the era. This is a very interesting museum, set in antique surroundings with tunnels, galleries and caves adding to the experience.

Jardin des Plantes

Address: 57 Rue Cuvier, 75005 Paris
Telephone: 01 40 79 56 04
Website: www.jardindesplantes.net
Open: 7 days per week from 07:30am to 5:30pm during winter, with closures at 8:00pm during the summer.
Rates: Access to the *Jardin des plantes*, Rose garden, Iris Garden and Botanical school garden are free for all. Entry to the Alpine garden is €2. Entry to the *grande serres* (large greenhouses) is €6 at full price, €4 for ages 4 to 16, and free for under 4s and disabled people.
Access: Métro Line 5 *Austerlitz* and Line 7 *Censier Daubenton- Jussieu* and Line 10 *Jussieu* / Bus Routes 24, 57, 61, 63, 67, 89 and 91

The *Jardin des Plantes* is the main botanical garden in Paris. It was founded in 1626 and covers 28 hectares. About 4,500 plants are housed here, arranged by type. 3 hectares are devoted to horticultural display. The *Jardins* have an Alpine garden with 3000 species from around the word. There is also a large Art Deco garden, Mexican and Australian greenhouses, and even a rose garden with 100 species of rose.

6th Arrondissement: Le Luxembourg

This arrondissement is home to the French Senate (the upper house of French parliament), the beautiful *St. Sulpice* Church and the stunning *Jardin du Luxembourg* and Palace. The Abbey of *Saint-Germain-des-Prés* is the heart of this area.

The 6th arrondissement is quintessential Paris, and is filled with designer boutiques and picturesque streets to walk around in. It has been home to famous artists such as Pablo Picasso, Oscar Wilde and Ernest Hemingway. Today it is one of Paris' most expensive areas to live in with about 45,000 inhabitants.

Jardin du Luxembourg

Address: Rue de Medicis & Rue de Vaugirard, 75006 Paris
Telephone: 01 42 34 23 62
Website: http://en.parisinfo.com/paris-museum-monument/71393/Jardin-du-Luxembourg
Open: 365 days a year. Hours depend on the season: Winter: 8:15 am to 4:30 pm and Summer: 7:30am to 9:30pm. Special hours during public holiday.
Rates: Free
Access: Métro Line 4 *Saint Sulpice* and Line 10 *Mabillon* / RER Line B *Luxembourg* / Bus Routes 21, 27, 38, 58, 82, 84, 85 and 89

Go for a stroll and a picnic, let the kids roam free, and enjoy the peace and quiet of nature in the buzz of the big city. With 21 hectares of landscape gardens, fountains, wide walkways, perfect photo spots, this is a favourite for families and couples wanting to get a bit of fresh air. A must see experience.

7th Arrondissement: Le Palais Bourbon

The 7th arrondissement is home to Paris' most famous landmark, The Eiffel Tower, as well as half a dozen of Paris' most famous museums. You could easily spend a few days in this arrondissment alone soaking in the culture and history.

This is historically where the upper class have chosen to take residence since the 7th century, and this still very much continues to be the case today.

The *Marché Saxe-Breteuil* (market) takes place on Thursdays and Saturdays between 7:00am and 3:00pm on *l'Avenue de Saxe*. Here, you are paying for quality, local produce. Prices are relatively expensive compared to other markets. It is also a lot less busy, however.

Musée Marmottan Monet

Address: 2 Rue Louis Boilly, 75007 Paris
Telephone: 01 44 96 50.33
Website: www.marmottan.fr/uk
Open: Tuesday to Sunday from 10:00am to 6:00pm, with a late closing on Thursday at 9:00pm. Closed Mondays.
Rates: Full rate - €11 / Reduced rate for under 18s and students under 25 - €6.50 / Free for children under 7 and disabled people.
Access: Métro Line 9 *La Muette* / RER Line C *Boulainvillers* / Bus Routes 22, 32, 52 and63

This museum offers a prestigious collection of Illumination works from the middle age to the Renaissance, as well as more contemporary artwork. Temporary exhibitions are regularly held on a variety of themes.

The Eiffel Tower

Address: 5 Avenue Anatole France, 75007 Paris

Telephone: 0892 701 239

Website: www.toureiffel.paris.fr

Open: 365 days a year. From mid-June to mid-September, the monument is open from 9:00am to 1:00am, and the rest of the year opening hours are from 9:30am to 11:00pm.

Rates: Adults over 24 (Lift to 2nd Floor - €11 / Lift to the top - €17 / Stairs to 2nd floor - €7), Ages 12 to 24 (Lift to 2nd Floor - €8.50 / Lift to the top - €14.50 / Stairs to 2nd floor - €5), Children 4 to 11, disabled people and their helpers (Lift to 2nd Floor - €4 / Lift to the top - €8 / Stairs to 2nd floor - €3)

Access: Métro Line 6 *Bir Hakeim* station or Line 9 *Trocadéro* station / RER Line C *Champ de Mars-Tour Eiffel* station / Bus Routes 82, 42, 87 and 69

Erected in 1889 for the Universal Exhibition and to celebrate the 100th anniversary of the French Revolution, the Eiffel Tower was originally a temporary structure destined to be demolished after 20 years. It was soon used to install radio transmitters, and it is still standing today.

At 324m tall, it dominates the Parisian skyline. Visited by almost 300 million people since its erection, it is one of the most visited monuments in the world and visitors quickly understand why once they stand at the top, 276m above the ground.

A visit to the Eiffel Tower is a multi-faceted trip. It is not merely a way to view the city from above, but an experience. Whether you climb to the first floor, second floor or all the way to the top this is an experience to savour.

A glass floor was recently installed on a section of the first floor of the tower allowing you to look directly down at the world below. Also on the first floor is an immersive projection show, displays to learn about the Tower, shops, the *58 Tour Eiffel* restaurant, and a buffet.

On the second level, you can get an even more incredible view of the city, try out the buffet, or experience the exquisite *Jules Verne* restaurant. Plus, learn about the construction and operation of the tower from the many exhibits.

Finally, for the most spectacular view, you need to take the lift to the top – here you will find two levels, one indoors and the other outdoors.

Be sure to pre-book your tickets online to avoid standing in the enormous queue lines for the ticket offices. You can either take a lift (elevator), or walk, to both the first and second floors. To reach the top you will take an elevator from the 2nd floor up. Here, you can take a look at Gustave Eiffel's office, explore the exhibits and savour a glass of bubbly from the champagne bar (between €12 and €21 per glass).

Musée Rodin

Address: 79 Rue de Varenne, 75007 Paris
Telephone: 01 44 18 61 10
Website: www.musee-rodin.fr
Open: Six days a week from 10:00am to 5:45pm (except Wednesday's late closing at 9:45pm). Closed Mondays, and on 1st January, 1st May and 25th December.
Rates: Full rate - €11.30 / Reduced rate (ages 18 to 25) - €8.30. Free entry for everyone on the first Sunday of each month, and under 18s year-round.
Access: Métro Line 13 *Varenne*, Lines 8 and 13 *Invalides* / RER Line C *Invalides* / Bus Routes 69, 82, 87 and 92

The Musée Rodin offers a collection of various sculptures by Rodin and Camille Claudel, as well as other artworks located in a magnificent building. The chapel and the gardens are also open to visit. The museum offers a very nice restaurant where you can enjoy the beautiful landscaping while having lunch.

Musée d'Orsay

Address: 1 Rue de La legion d'honneur, 75007 Paris
Telephone: 01 40 49 48 14
Website: www.musee-orsay.fr
Open: From Tuesday to Sunday from 9:30am to 6:00pm (except Thursdays when the museum closes late at 9:45pm). Closed every Monday, 1st May and 25th December.
Rates: Acces to Orsay and Orangerie Museums - €16 / Access to Musee d'Orsay - €11 / Free for under 18s
Access: Métro Lines 1, 2 *Solferino* / RER Line C *Musee d'Orsay* / Bus Routes 24, 63, 68, 69, 73, 83, 84 and 94, Balabus *Cité* stop.

Installed in 1986 in what was previously the 86 year-old Orsay train station, the Musée d'Orsay is home to a very large collection of artwork, ranging from classic and contemporary paintings to sculptures, achitecture and even graphic arts.

On the ground floor be sure to take a look at paintings by Delacroix, Edgar Degas and Ingres. Manet's famous *Le déjeuner sur l'herbe* (lunch on the grass) is also here. The top floor has entire galleries devoted to Monet and Renoir, and The Terrace filled with sculptures; an entire area is dedicated to Rodin.

The €6 per person, Masterpieces of the Musée d'Orsay tour covers an overview of the museum's collections in 1 hour 30 minutes.

Musée de l'armée - Les Invalides

Address: 6 Boulevard des Invalides, 75007 Paris
Telephone: 08 10 11 33 99
Website: www.musee-armee.fr
Open: Open seven days a week. Closed 1st January, 1st May and 25th December. Open 10:00am to 5:00pm from November to March, and 10:00am to 6:00pm from April to October. Certain sections of the musuem may be closed on the first Monday of each month.
Rates: Full rate - €9.50 / Reduced rate - €7.50 / Free for under 18s, disabled people, and for Europeen resident under 26.
Access: Métro Line 8 *Invalides* or *Tour Maubourg* and Line 13 *Varennes* or *Invalides* / RER Line C *Invalides* / Bus Routes 28, 63, 69, 82, 83, 92 and 93

From arms through the ages, to Napoléon I's tomb, and even a special section dedicated to armour between the 13th and the 17th centuries, all kinds of weaponry can be seen here. There are actual weapons on display, as well as paintings depicting weapons and war scenes. A special section is entirely dedicated to Charles de Gaulle. Everything you want to know about army and war can be found here.

Napoleon I's tomb is located in the Dome Church portion of Les Invalides.

Musée du Quai Branly

Address: 37 Quai Branly, 75007 Paris
Telephone: 01 56 61 70 00
Website: www.quaibranly.fr/en
Open: Tues to Sun. Closed Mondays, 1st May and 25th December. 11:00am to 7:00pm on Tues, Wed and Sun. Closes two hours later on other days.
Rates: Full rate - €9 / Reduced rate - €7 / Free for under 18s, EU residents 18 to 25, and disabled people.
Access: Métro Line 6 *Bir Hakeim*, Line 8 *Ecole Militaire* and Line 9 *Alma-Marceau* or *Iéna* / RER Line C *Pont de l'Alma* or *Champs de Mars* / Bus Routes 42, 63, 68, 72, 80, 82 and 92

From African artifacts to Asian silk, this museum about arts and civilisation will help you link the two through art, objects and the various documentation. The audioguide available in various languages is particularly well designed.

Pont Alexandre III

Address: Pont Alexandre III, Quay D'Orsay, 75007 Paris
Open: Public area, open all the time
Access: Metro Line 13 or 8 *Invalides* / Bus Routes 63, 83 and 93

The Pont Alexandre III is one of the most emblematic bridges in Paris. It was inaugurated for the 1900 Paris World's Fair. At its four extremities are 17 metres-high structures crowned with gilt bronze sculptures representing arts, sciences, commerce and industry. Enjoy a sweeping view of the *Invalides*, the *Petit Palais* and *Grand Palais*, as well as the Eiffel Tower.

8th Arrondissement: L'Elysée

The 8th arrondissement is one of the main business districts in Paris, and is today home to the Champs Elysées, one of Paris' most recognisable hotspots. Many luxurious hotels are located in the 8th district. It is also a political hotspot due to it being home to the Ministry of the Interior (which deals with the country's security and immigration) and the *Palais de l'Elysée* (the official residence of France's president). This arrondissement contains many famous Parisian landmarks.

Musée Jacquemart-André

Address: 158 Boulevard Haussmann, 75008 Paris
Telephone: 01 45 62 11 59
Website: www.musee-jacquemart-andre.com/en/
Open: Every day, including public holidays from 10:00am to 6:00pm, with a late closing on Mondays and Saturdays until 8:30pm during exhibitions.
Rates: Full rate - €12 / Reduced rate for under 18s and students under 25 - €10 / Free for children under 7 and disabled people
Access: Métro Line 9 *Saint Augustin, Miromesnil*, Line 13 *Saint Philippe du Roule* / RER Line A *Charles de Gaulle Etoile* / Bus Routes 22, 28, 43, 52, 54, 80, 83, 84 and 93

The museum was once the private home of the *Jacquemart-Andrés* family. They spent much of their fortune on a collection of fine arts. This space is now a museum, filled with paintings, sculptures, and objects of all sorts. Here you can discover a refined universe of art, with flamboyant décor around the mansion.

Arc de Triomphe

Address: Place Charles de Gaulle, 75008 Paris
Telephone: 01 55 37 73 77
Website: http://arc-de-triomphe.monuments-nationaux.fr
Open: Daily except 1st January, 1st May, 8th May in the morning, 14th July in the morning, 11th November in the morning, and 25th December. Open from 10:00am to 11:00pm from April to September, and 10:00am to 10:30pm from October to March.
Rates: Adults over 18 - € 9.50 / Under 18 - € 6 / Groups (min 20 adults) - € 7.50 / Under 18 - Free accompanied by parent(s) / 18-25 year old citizen of the EU - Free / Disabled persons and their helpers - Free
Access: Métro Lines 1, 2 & 6 *Charles de Gaulle Etoile* station / RER Line A *Charles de Gaulle Etoile* station / Bus Routes 22, 30, 31, 52, 73 and 92, Balabus *Charles de Gaulle Etoile* stop

Built between 1806 and 1836, following Napoléon's orders, the *Arc de Triomphe* is 50m high and 45m wide, and dominates the centre of the famous roundabout *Place Charles de Gaulle* (historically known as *Place de l'Etoile*). Here twelve of Paris' major avenues originate. The area is now home to the tomb of the unknown soldier and the eternal flame in memory of all the soldiers who died in combat. The flame is revived every day at 6:30pm usually by representatives of veterans associations. Both the tomb and the eternal flame are located on the bottom of the arch and accessible without paying admission.

Access to the area around the arch is free year-round. Entry into the museum inside the arch is payable.

Avenue des Champs-Elysées

Address: Avenue des Champs-Elysées, 75008 Paris
Open: 24/7, 365 days a year
Rates: Public area – open all the time
Access: Métro Lines 1, 2 & 6 *Charles de Gaulle Etoile* station / RER Line A *Charles de Gaulle Etoile* station / Bus Routes 22, 30, 31, 52, 73 and 92, Balabus: *Charles de Gaulle Etoile* stop

One of Paris' most famous hotspots, the *Champs-Elysées* boasts beautiful views, luxury (and high-street) shopping and restaurants for all tastes and budgets. The avenue runs from *Place de la Concorde* to *Place de Charles de Gaulle Etoile*, so a walk along the road will take you from one famous location to another. Around Christmas-time the area hosts markets along the wide pavements.

Americans, in particular, should look for number 92 where Thomas Jefferson once lived – a plaque here remembers this.

Place de la Concorde

Address: Place de la Concorde, 75008 Paris
Open: Public area – open all the time
Rates: Free
Access: Métro Lines 1, 8 & 12 *Concorde* station / RER Line A *Concorde* station / Bus Routes 24, 42, 52, 72, 73, 84 and 94, Balabus *Concorde* stop

Built between 1755 and 1775, the *Place de la Concorde* has been the place of many events in the history of Paris, including the beheading of King Louis XVI. In its centre stands the Obélisque, gift of the Vice King of Egypt to King Charles X of France. It is a magnificent piece of Egyptian art decorated with gold hieroglyphs. From the *Place de la Concorde* one can enjoy superbs views all over the adjacent streets.

Musée du Petit Palais

Address: Avenue Winston Churchill, 75008 Paris
Telephone: 01 53 43 40 00
Website: www.petitpalais.paris.fr
Open: Tuesday to Sunday from 10:00am to 6:00pm. Closed every Monday and on public holidays.
Rates: The permanent collection is free admission. Temporary exhibitions are priced from €5 to €11. Reduced tariffs are available for temporary exhibitions.
Access: Métro Lines 1 & 13 *Champs Elysées – Clemenceau* / RER Line A *Charles de Gaulle-Etoile* or Line C *Invalides* / Bus Routes 28, 42, 72, 73, 83 and 93

This historical building is now used as a museum. It is the museum of fine arts of the City of Paris. From Baroque themed exhibitions to concerts and films, this museum offers a wide variety of collections. One of our favourite things is that generally this museum is not hugely crowded, making visits a pleasure.

Musée du Grand Palais

Address: 3 Avenue du General Eisenhower, 75008 Paris
Telephone: 01 44 13 17 17
Website: www.grandpalais.fr
Open: Six days a week from 10:00am to 8:00pm (depending on the exhibition). Closed on Tuesdays and public holidays.
Rates: Depends on the exhibition – usually starts at €11.
Access: Métro Lines 1 & 13 *Champs Elyses – Clemenceau* and Line 9 *Franklin Roosevelt* / RER Line C *Invalides* / Bus Routes 28, 42, 52, 63, 72, 73, 80, 83 and 93 / Batobus: *Champs Elysées*

Located in the same building as the *Palais de la Découverte*, the Museum of the Grand Palais offers regular and varied exhibitions of all sorts. From fashion to modern art, and sculptures to grand receptions and openings, this magnificent building is well worth a visit. Pop in next door and discover all there is to know about science at the *Palais de la Découverte*.

Bateaux Mouche

Address: Port de la Conference – Pont de L'Alma, 75008 Paris
Telephone: 01 42 25 96 10
Website: www.bateaux-mouches.fr
Open: 365 days a year. Hours depend on the season – generally 10:15am to 10:30pm with departures every 15 minutes in high season and every hour in low season.
Rates: Adults - €13.50 / Children aged 4 to 12 - €5.50 / Under 4s travel free / There are also special lunch and night dinner cruise options available.
Access: Metro Line 1 *Franklin Roosevelt* and Line 9 *Alma Marceau* / RER Line C *Pont de L'Alma* / Bus Routes 28, 42, 49, 63, 72, 80, 83 and 92

You cannot visit Paris without doing a cruise on the famous "Bateaux-Mouche". These strange looking ships go up and down the Seine river, taking you through on an interesting journey across Paris. On board, you will get to see many landmarks from a unique angle. Cruises last about 1 hour 10 minutes.

Parc Monceau

Address: 30 Boulevard de Courcelles, 75008 Paris
Telephone: 01 42 27 39 56
Open: Daily from 7:00am to 9:00pm, and to 10:00pm in the summer.
Rates: Free
Access: Métro Line 2 *Monceau* / Bus Routes 30 and 84

Built in the 17ᵗʰ century, *Parc Monceau* is one of the most elegant gardens in Paris. You will find many surprises, such as numerous statues, renaissance archways, spectacular trees, a large pond, a variety of birds and a playground. *Parc Monceau* is a peaceful, pleasant park visited by both parisians and tourists. It is a mere ten minutes from the *Champs Elysées*, yet it feels a world away.

Eglise de la Madeleine

Address: Place de la Madeleine, 75008 Paris
Telephone: 01 44 5169 00
Open: Daily from 9:30am to 7:00pm
Rates: Free
Access: Métro Lines 8, 12 and 14 *La Madeleine* / RER Line A *Auber* / Bus Routes 24, 42, 43, 52, 84 and 94

The *Madeleine* is a Catholic church situated near *Place de la Concorde*. Its construction began in 1764, and was stopped several times. It was even demolished during the revolution. The current church, from 1842, is neo-classical style in and is a temple in glory to Napoleon's army. It is inspired by *Maison Carrée* in Nîmes, one of the best preserved old Roman temples.

9th Arrondissement: L'Opéra

This arrondissement is known as one of the city's financial hubs, housing many French banks' headquarters. It is also one of the arts centres of the capital, containing many cinemas, as well as the stunning *Opéra* theatre. The *Boulevard Haussman* is home to large department stores *Galeries Lafayette* and *Printemps*. It is one of the city's easiest areas to reach by metro, as there as 19 stations in the area.

Eglise Notre Dame de Lorette

Address: 1 Rue Flechier / 9 Rue de Chataudun, 75009 Paris
Telephone: 01 48 78 92 72
Open: Daily from 7:30am to 7:30pm on weekdays, and from 9:00am to midday and 2:30pm to 7:30pm on weekends.
Rates: Free
Access: Métro Line 12 *Notre Dame de Lorette* / Bus Routes 26, 32, 42, 43, 67, 74 and 85

Notre Dame de Lorette is a Neoclassical church. Its construction was completed in 1836, 13 years after its beginning. Instead of decorative paintings being placed on the church's walls, murals were painted directly onto them. The facade features six angels in adoration before the Madonna and child. Inside are statues that represent the theological virtues of charity, hope and faith.

Musée Grévin

Address: 10 Boulevard Montmartre 75009 Paris
Telephone: 01 47 70 85 05
Website: www.grevin-paris.com
Open: Every day, except the last week of September when the museum is closed. Opening times vary on different days and seasons.
Rates: Full tariff - €24.50 / 15 to 17 years old - €21.50 / 6 to 14 years old - €17.50 / Free for under 6s.
Access: Métro Lines 8 and 9 *Grands Boulevards* / Bus Routes 20, 39, 48, 67, 74 and 85

Musée Grévin is a waxwork museum created in the 19th century by journalist Arthur Meyer. His idea was simple: to create a place where the public could see wax figures of well-known people. It was an instant success.

Today, inside a completely renovated museum, you will experience the spirit of Paris with scenes from the 20th century's major events, French history and newer additions. 300 figures are waiting to meet you from Marie-Antoinette to Michael Jackson, and Louis XVI to Obélix. Think of it as Paris' version of Madame Tussauds.

Opéra Garnier (Palais Garnier)

Address: 8 Rue Scribe, 75009 Paris
Telephone: 08 92 89 90 90
Website: www.operadeparis.fr
Open: The monument is open every day, except 1st January and 1st May.
Open from 10:00am to 6:00pm from 15th July to 31st August, and 10:00am to
5:00pm the rest of the year. Performance times vary. See the calendar at
www.operadeparis.fr/en/calendrier
Rates: For a tour of the building: €11 per adult over 18 / €7 for students and
under-25s / Free for under 12s, disabled people and their helpers. For the
shows – From €10 to €213 depending on the seat and show.
Access: Métro Lines 3, 7 & 8 *Opéra* station, Lines 7 & 9 *Chaussée d'Antin*
station and Lines 8 & 14 *Madeleine* station / RER Line A *Auber* station / Bus
Routes 20, 21, 2, 27, 29, 42, 52, 66, 68, 81 and 95 *Opéra* stop.

A French institution since the first stone was laid in 1862, the *Opéra Garnier* is
as much a historical monument as it is a ballet and concert venue. Whether
you choose to enjoy the outside and watch life go by, or take a tour of the
inside, this is a must-see while in Paris.

The famous *Opéra Garnier* is a gem of architecture, that can be visited when
showing are not playing. Attending either a ballet or a concert here is a special
experience of a lifetime, the combinaition of art and architecture in
astonishing décor.

10th Arrondissement: L'Enclos Saint Laurent

This arrondissement is known for housing two of Paris' largest railway stations – *Gare du Nord* and *Gare de l'Est*. It is one of Paris' most populous districts with 100,000 inhabitants. A large part of the Canal Saint Martin is in this area.

Canal Saint Martin

Address: Canal Saint Martin, Quai de Valmy, 75010 Paris
Open: Public area - open all the time
Rates: Free
Access: Métro Lines 2, 5 and 7 *Jaurès* and Line 7 *Louis Blanc* / Bus Routes: 26, 46 and 48

Canal Saint Martin is a 4.5-kilometre-long canal connecting *Canal de L'Ourq* to the river *Seine* running underground between *Bastille* and *République*. The canal with its tree shaded quays, iron bridges and its unusual hydraulic lift bridge (dating back to 1885) is a popular destination for Parisians and tourists. There are several popular restaurants and cafés, as well as picnic areas on the quay.

11th and 12th Arrondissements: Popincourt and Reuilly

The 11th arrondissement is one of the most densely populated areas in all of Europe, with over 150,000 inhabitants in a mere 3.67km². The *Boulevard Richard-Lenoir* is home to one of Paris' largest fruit and vegetable markets. The 12th arrondissement has a similar population and contains the *Bois de Vincennes*. The areas are especially famous for the historical *Place de la Bastille*.

Zoo de Vincennes

Address: Route de la Ceinture du Lac, 75012 Paris
Telephone: 08 11 22 41 22
Website: www.parczoologiquedeparis.fr
Opening Days: Open 365 days a year from 10:00am to 6:00pm (with an early closing at 5:00pm during the winter)
Rates: Full rate - €22, from 12 to 25 years old - €16.50, from 3 to 11 years old - €14, and disabled people and under 3s enter free of charge.
Access: Métro Line 1 *Saint Mande* and Line 8 *Porte Doree* / Bus Routes 46, 86 and 325 / Tramway Line T3 *Porte Doree*

Located in the Bois de Vincennes, the 80 years old *Parc Zoologique de Paris (Zoo de Vincennes)* was completly rebuilt from 2008 to 2014, and is now divided into five geographical zones (Sahel, Patagonia, Europe, Amazonia, Madagascar) where animals live in recreations of their original habitat. The zoo is a pleasant and interesting attraction. The zoo's icon is a 65 metre-tall rocky hill called "Grand Rocher".

Place de la Bastille

Address: Place de la Bastille, 75011 Paris
Website: http://paris1900.lartnouveau.com/paris12/la_bastille
Open: Public area – open all the time
Rates: Free
Access: Métro Lines 1, 5 and 8 *Bastille* station/ Noctilien Routes N01, N02, N11, N16 and N144 / Bus Routes 20, 29, 65, 69, 76, 86, 87 and 91, Balabus *Cité* stop

The *Place de la Bastille* is a square in Paris where the « royal » Bastille prison was erected, this old defensive castle was transformed into a state prison by Richelieu in the 17th century. For the French people and more particularly Parisians, this prison was a symbol of horror, and oppression of the royal autocratic cruelty.

La Bastille was stormed and completely destroyed on the 14th of July 1789 during the French revolution. In the middle of the square the July column was erected to commemorate the events of the 1830 July revolution (the second French revolution). Today this square is home to concerts, political meetings and events. The north eastern of the Bastille area is famous for its nightlife with famous restaurants, cafés, bars and concert halls.

Opéra Bastille

Address: Place de la Bastille, 75009 Paris
Telephone: 08 92 89 90 90 (Booking from France) / + 33 1 71 25 24 23 (booking from overseas)
Website: www.operadeparis.fr/en/
Open: Depends on performances. See the calendar at www.operadeparis.fr/en/calendrier
Rates: From €10 to €213 depending the show and seat. Tours of the building cost: €12 per adult / €10 for students and under 25s / €6 for under 10s.
Access: Métro Lines 1, 5 and 8 *Bastille* / RER A *Gare de Lyon* / Bus Routes 20, 29, 65, 69, 76, 86, 87 and 91

The new version of the French Opéra, the *Opéra Bastille* is a gem of modern technology, offering what has been called "almost perfect" acoustics. Modern and innovative equipment, several halls and amphitheatres make this a modern and versatile arts venue.

With interesting architecture, this is a fascinating place to explore, with tours taking you behind the scenes where you will find out the ins and outs of the various sets.

13th and 14th Arrondissements: Les Gobelins and L'Observatoire

The 13th arrondissement is known for its Asian communities, with many Chinese and Viatnamese people having settled in the area. The population in this area keeps expanding, with over 185,000 locals here. The new *Paris Rive Gauche* business area is also making this one of the city's business hotspots. The 14th arrondissement is also the traditional home of the city's artists.

The Catacombes

Address: Avenue du Colonel Henri Rol-Tanguy, 75014 Paris
Telephone: 01 43 22 47 63
Website: www.catacombes.paris.fr
Open: Tuesday to Sunday from 10:00am to 8:00pm. Closed on 1st May.
Rates: Adults: € 10 / Ages 18 to 26: € 8 / Under 18s, disabled people: free
Access: Metro Line 4 and 6 *Denfert Rochereau* station / RER Line B *Denfert Rochereau* station / Bus Routes 38 and 68
Additional Information: The total walking path is 2kms, with the overall visit taking about 45 minutes. The temperature inside is 14°C. Children under 14 must be accompanied by an adult. A 30-minute audioguide costs €5.

Chosen in 1785 to accommodate the remains of the *Cimetière des Innocents* the authorities decided to close for health reasons, this old quarry was chosen for its existing tunnels and caves. Until 1814, remains of Paris' cemeteries were brought here. Today, the *Catacombes* are well known, and the countless legends around them add to the mystery of the place.

15th and 16th Arrondissements: Vaugirard and Passy

The 15th arrondissement today contains the *Tour Montparnasse*, one of the city's tallest skyscrapers that provides a view over the city from its observation levels. This is the most populous district in the city, with about 240,000 people living here.

The 16th arrondissement is filled with famous museums, and is home to some of the city's most expensive and luxurious residences.

Musée d'Art Moderne de la Ville de Paris (Paris Modern Art Museum)

Address: 11 Avenue du President Wilson, 75116 Paris
Telephone: 01 53 67 40 00
Website: www.mam.paris.fr
Open: Tues to Sun 10:00am to 6:00pm, 10:00pm on Thurs. Closed Mons, 1st Jan, 20th Apr, 1st & 8th May, 14th Jul, 15th Aug, 1st & 11th Nov and 25th Dec.
Rates: Permanent collection is free. Temporary exhibitions are €5 to €11, 50% discount for ages 14 to 26. Under 14s and disabled people enter free.
Access Métro Line 9 *Alma - Marceau* or *Iéna* / RER Line C *Pont de l'Alma* / Bus Routes 32, 42, 72, 80, 82 and 92

A mix of classic and modern looks, this building is home to an almost 10,000 strong collection of modern artwork from the 20th and 21st centuries.

Musée National de la Marine

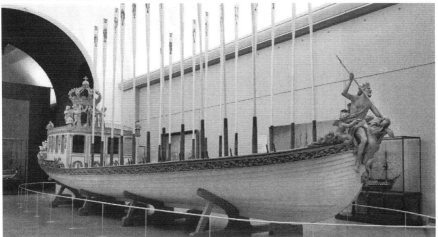

Address: 17 Place du Trocadero, 75116 Paris
Telephone: 01 53 65 69 53
Website: www.musee-marine.fr/paris
Open: Six days a week from 11:00am to 6:00pm. Closed Tuesdays and 1st
January, 1st May and 25th December.
Rates: Full tariff - €8.50 for the permanent collection and €10 for permanent
and temporary exhibitions. Reduced tariffs are also available.
Access: Métro Lines 6 & 9 *Trocadéro* / Bus Routes 22, 30, 32, 63, 72 and 82

Ship models, replicas of famous vesels, and life-size parts take you into the
world of marines from around the world. Learn about the evolution of
maritime equpiment over the years, war vessels, etc… in enquisite décor.

Musée du Jeu de Paume

Address: 1 Place de la Concorde, 75116 Paris
Telephone: 01 47 03 12 50
Website: www.jeudepaume.org
Open: Six days a week from 11:00am to 7:00pm, late closing on Tuesdays at
9:00pm. Closed Mondays and 1st May and 25th December
Rates: Adults - €10 / Under 12s & disabled– free / Reduced rate - €7.50
Access: Métro Lines 1, 8 & 12 *Concorde* / Bus Routes 24, 42, 72, 73, 84 & 94

All types of visual arts, from paintings to live performances to modern
sculptures, are given a home in mostly temporary exhibitions at the *Musée du
Jeu de Paume*. The building is in peaceful surroundings and well worth a visit.

Bois de Boulogne

Address: Bois de Boulogne, 750016 Paris
Website: http://en.parisinfo.com/paris-museum-monument/71494/Bois-de-Boulogne
Open: The Forest side is open 24/7, 365 days a year. Opening times for the *Jardin d'Acclimatation, Jardin des Serres d'Auteuil* and *Parc Bagatelle* depend on the season. They open between 8:00am and 9:00am and close between 6:00pm and 8:30pm
Rates: Free access to the forest and *Jardin des serres d'Auteuil. Jardin d'Acclimatation* - €3 / Bagatelle - €5.50 / Boat Hire - €10 per hour
Access: Métro Line 1 *Les Sablons* and Line 2 *Porte Dauphine* and Line 10 *Porte d'Auteuil* / Bus Routes 32, 52, 63, 73, 82, 241 and 244, Balabus.

Once a royal hunting ground, the *Bois de Boulogne* has become the largest relaxation spot in the west of Paris since it was transformed and designed by Baron Haussman. There is a lot to see including *Parc Bagatelle, le Jardin des Serres d'Auteuil, le Jardin d'Acclimatation*, the *Louis Vuitton* foundation building, the famous *Rolland Garros* stadium and *Auteuil* horse racing. Spanning 865 hectares, with 28 kilometres of walkways and 15 kilometres of cycles routes, a lake and numerous facilities *le Bois de Boulogne* is an unmissable experience.

17th and 18th Arrondissements: Les Batignolles-Monceau and La Butte Montmartre

The 17th arrondissement is a large arrondissement filled with embassies and consulates from around the world. The 18th arrondissement is known for the district of Monmartre and its basilica. It is Paris' second most populous area and is quickly being gentrified.

Basilique du Sacré-Coeur

Address: 36 Rue du Chevalier de la Barre, 75018 Paris
Telephone: 01 53 41 89 00
Website: www.sacre-coeur-montmartre.com
Open: 7 days a week from 6:00am to 10:30pm
Rates: Free
Access: Métro Line 2 *Pigalles* and Line 12 *Jules Joffrin - Pigalles* / Bus Routes 30, 51, 80 and 85

The *Sacré-Coeur* is a Roman catholic church situated at the summit of the *Butte Montmartre*, the highest point in the city. Built between 1875 and 1914, the *Sacré-Coeur* is made of travertine stone, which constantly exudes calcite ensuring the basilica remains white even with weathering and pollution. The mosaic in the Apse, "Christ in Majesty", is among the largest in the world.

The basilica's complex includes a garden for meditation with a fountain. The top of the dome is open to tourists offering a panoramic view of Paris. You do not even need to climb up to the dome, just the city view from the church's steps will blow you away – but the extra climb will make the experience even better.

Montmartre Cemetery

Address: 20 Avenue Rachel, 75018 Paris
Telephone: 01 53 42 36 30
Open: 7 days per week. From 8:00am to 5:30pm or 6:00pm Mondays to Saturday, and 9:00am to 5:30pm or 6:00pm on Sundays and public holidays.
Rates: Free
Access: Métro Line 2 & 13 *Place Clichy* / Bus Lines 30, 74, 80, 95

Montmartre Cemetry was opened in January 1825. It is located on an old gypsum quarry which was used during the French revolution as a mass grave. Montmartre Cemetry is the final resting place of many famous artists such as *Sartre* and *Baudelaire* (a map with names is available at the cemetry entrance). It is a popular tourist destination.

19th Arrondissement: Les Buttes Chaumont

The 19th arrondissement is famous for the two large parks: *Parc des Buttes Chaumont* and *Parc de la Villette*. The *Conservatoire de Paris*, one of the most well-known music schools is located here too.

Musée Cité des Sciences et de l'Industrie

Address: 30 Avenue Corantin Cariou, 75019 Paris
Telephone: 01 40 05 80 00
Website: www.cite-sciences.fr
Open: From Tuesday to Sunday from 10:00am to 6:00pm, with a late closing at 7:00pm on Sundays. Closed every Monday, and 1st May and 25th December.
Rates: Full rate - €12 / Reduced rate - €10 / Children under 6 - €6 / Submarine access - €3
Access: Métro Line 7 *Porte de la Villette* / Tramway Line T3B *Porte de la Villette* / Bus Routes 139, 150 and 152

This museum has a large offer of science exhibits and experiments in a user-friendly environment, making science fun and accessible to all. Everything is covered here, from the history of scientific discoveries to today's modern achievements. Temporary exhibitions are constantly renewed, ensuring that there is always something of interest to everyone no matter their age. A must-do for adults, children of all ages and an unforgettable family outing.

Parc des Buttes Chaumont

Address: 1 Rue Botzaris, 75019 Paris
Telephone: 01 48 03 83 10
Website: http://en.parisinfo.com/paris-museum-monument/71468/Parc-des-Buttes-Chaumont
Open: 365 days a year. Hours depend on the season: 7:00am to 8:00pm in winter and 7:00am to 10:00pm in summer.
Rates: Free
Access: Métro Line 7 *Botzaris – Buttes Chaumont* and Line 5 *Laumière* / Bus Routes 26, 48, 60 and 75

Buttes Chaumont is one of the largest parks in Paris (25 hectares); its landscape is a blend of English and Chinese style and is a unique sight in the city. This park was opened in 1867 for the world's fair, it was designed by the architect Davioud who transformed the old quarries by digging out a lake with a rocky island in the middle, and creating a cave featuring artificial stalactics as well as waterfalls and brooks.

20th Arrondissement: Ménilmontant

The 20th arrondissement is home to 200,000 people and is known for its large immigrant population. Its most recognised landmark is the *Père Lachaise Cemetery.*

Père Lachaise Cemetery

Address: 16 Rue Repos, 75020 Paris
Telephone: 01 55 25 82 10
Website: www.pere-lachaise.com
Open: Daily, 8:00am to 5:30pm or 6:00pm Monday to Saturday, and 9:00am to 5:30pm or 6:00pm Sundays and public holidays.
Rates: Free
Access: Métro Line 3 *Gambetta* / Bus Routes 60, 69 ans 102

Père Lachaise is one of the most well known and widely visited cemeteries in the world, with over 3 million annual visitors. It is also the largest cemetery in Paris, measuring 44 hectares. The cemetery takes its name from the confessor of Louis XIV, *Père Francois de la Chaise*.

The cemetery was established in 1804 by Napoleon. *Père Lachaise* is a green area with beautiful trees, and graves which range from a simple headstone to towering monuments and even mini chapels. Many well-known names have their graves in *Père Lachaise* (including Oscar Wilde, Chopin, Jim Morisson, Edith Piaf and more). The best way to enjoy your visit at *Père Lachaise* is to stroll along its shaded alleys and happen upon the different graves.

Further Afield:

If you want to travel outside the main city of Paris (intra-murros), you can find many delights just a short journey away.

Disneyland Paris

Address: Disneyland Paris, 77777 Marne-la-Vallée
Telephone: 0825 30 0530
Website: www.disneylandparis.com/
Open: 365 days a year. Opening hours vary by season from 10:00am to 6:00pm in low season to 10:00am to 11:00pm in high season.
Rates: Rates depend on how far in advance a ticket is purchased. Gate prices are €75 for a one-park, one-day adult ticket and €90 for a two-park, one-day adult ticket. Children ages 3 to 11 inclusive pay a few euros less per person. Children under 3 go free. Book online in advance for discounts.
Access: RER Line A Marne la Vallee – Chessy (40 minutes from central Paris) / Shuttles from airports to the park's entrance via www.magicalshuttle.fr / Daily shuttles from Paris Gare du Nord; Opera, Madeleine, Chatelet / Marne la Vallee – Chessy TGV Station

Not only for children, adults can have fun too at Disneyland Paris. From magical journeys through the various attractions to parades, character meets and fireworks, there is fun for everyone. It can take several days to see all the resort has to offer, with its two theme parks, its shopping and dining district, and numerous resort hotels to explore.

If you will be visiting the resort be sure to purchase *The Independent Guide to Disneyland Paris 2016* (the number 1 book on the resort) to greatly enhance your experience and minimise your spending and time waiting in queue lines.

Parc Asterix

Address: Park Asterix, 60128 Plailly
Telephone: 08 26 46 66 26
Website: http://www.parcasterix.fr/en
Open: Seasonally. In 2016, the park is open most days from 2nd April to 2nd November. Open from 10:00am to 6:00pm except for special events, and busier days when the park closes later.
Rates: Gate prices are €47 for a one-day adult ticket / €39 for children 3 to 11 / Children under 3 go free.
Access: From Paris: RER Line B from *Gare du Nord* to *Charles de Gaulle airport*, then a short shuttle bus from Terminal 1 and 3 (tickets from the Parc Asterix counter) / Shuttle every morning departing at 09:00am from *Le Louvre Palais Royal* (€23 return ticket), returning at 6:30pm from the park / By road: The park is situated 30km north of Paris via the A1 motor way (parking is €10 Euro per day).

The famous French cartoon characters Astérix and Obélix have their own theme park. Enjoy the rides based on the various Astérix and Obélix adventures themes, meet characters from different stories, watch the shows, and have a day to remember. Fun for all!

Chateau de Versailles / Versailles Palace

Address: Château de Versailles, Place d'Armes, 78000 Versailles

Telephone: 01 30 83 78 00

Website: http://en.chateauversailles.fr

Open: April to October: Palace open every day except Monday from 9:00am to 6:30pm, Gardens 8:00am to 8:30pm. November to March: Palace open every day except Monday 9:00am to 5:30pm, Gardens 8:00am to 6:00pm.

Rates: 1 day ticket including gardens and daytime fountain shows is €18, and €25 for 2 days. A palace-only ticket is €15 or €13 for concessions. Nighttime fountain show tickets are €24 per person (€20 reduced rate). Gardens-only tickets are €8 (€7 reduced rate). Under 18s, EU residents under 26, disabled people and an accompanying adult enter the palace for free (gardens and nighttime fountain shows are still payable, however).

Access: RER C *Versailles Rive Gauche* / SNCF trains *Versailles Chantiers* or *Versailles Rive Droite* / Versailles Express coach from Eiffel Tower.

This luxurious palace, located 20 kilometres from central Paris, has intriguing and stunning details just waiting to be discovered around every corner. The Hall of Mirrors, the *Opéra* and the Chapel are particular highlights. The palace was the centre of politics in France from 1682 until the French revolution in 1789. An audio guide is included in your admission ticket.

Strolls around the gardens are sure to inspire. The musical fountain shows take place on weekends and other days between late March and early November. Breath-taking night time fountain shows include fireworks and lasers, and are played on Saturdays from mid-June to mid-September.

Dining: Restaurants in Paris

Paris is one of the culinary capitals of the world, and French food is renowned worldwide. The focus in France is "homemade" and "fresh" meaning that, generally speaking, food is fresh and made in-house with local ingredients. Quality really is important to the discerning French clientele.

As well as full-service meals, you will find a variety of fast-food establishments (though 'fast' is not necessarily what we would call them) from national chains to worldwide behemoths.

No trip to Paris would be complete without a typical French snack including *gauffres, macarrons* (*Ladurée* being the go to place for these) and *crêpes*. Local *boulangeries* (bakeries) offer tasty baguettes, as well as *pains au chocolat,* and *croissants*. Locations around major tourist attractions usually serve these treats, but with a hefty mark-up.

Your trip should also include a visit to one of Paris' many *cafés* for a taste of the local's coffee, as well as sandwiches and light bites. For American coffee chain lovers, you will be disappointed to know that Starbucks locations are nowhere near as common as in other European locations such as London – there are still, however, about 50 locations in Paris.

Gratuities (a.k.a, tips) are included in the price of your meal, though these will not necessarily go to your server. By law, servers are all paid at least the minimum wage. If you enjoy your meal, it is still nice to tip a few euros.

Note that like in many European capitals, it is common for restaurants to close between their lunch and dinner service. A la carte prices stated in this section are for mains only.

1st Arrondissement

LE LOUVRE RIPAILLE
Wine bar, restaurant and bistro, ideally situated close to the *Musée du Louvre,* this is the perfect setting for a Parisian lunch or dinner.
Address: 1 Rue Perrault, 75001 Paris
Telephone: 01 42 97 49 91
Access: Métro Line 1 *Louvre - Rivoli* station
Open: Lunch: Mon to Sat 12:00 to 14:30. Dinner: Mon to Sat 19:30 to 23:00.
Pricing: Set menu: €19. A la carte: €9.80 to €25.

LES VOYELLES

Restaurant, bistro and bar, this establishment offers drinks and snacks, as well as sit down dinners in the heart of Ile de la Cité, for a true French experience.

Address: 74 Quai des Orfèvres, 75001 Paris
Telephone: 01 46 33 69 75
Access: Métro Line 7 – *Pont Neuf* station
Open: Tuesday to Saturday from 10:30am to midnight.
Pricing: Set menu lunch: €17. Set menu dinner: €30. A la carte: €9.50 to €21.50.

BRASSERIE DU LOUVRE

Warm wood finishes, modern traditional cuisine and beautiful views onto the Louvre from the terrace.

Address: Place du Palais Royal, 75001 Paris
Telephone: 01 73 11 12 34
Access: Métro Line 7 *Palais Royal* station and Line 14 *Pyramides* station
Open: 12:00 noon to 22:00
Pricing: A la carte: €16 to €33.

AU PIED DE COCHON

Open 24/7, *Au Pied de Cochon* offers meals throughout the day and night. With a varied menu, ranging from fresh seafood to French charcuterie, there is something for everyone.

Address: 6 Rue Coquillère, 75001 Paris
Telephone: 01 40 13 77 00
Access: Métro Line 1 *Louvre - Rivoli* station and Line 2 *Les Halles* station and Lines 7, 11 & 14 *Châtelet* station / RER Lines A, B & D *Châtelet - Les Halles* station
Open: Every day – 24 hours a day
Pricing: Set breakfast menu: € 6.10. Standard menu: € 35.50. Children's menu: €11. A la carte: €9 to €49.90.

LE BAUDELAIRE

Enjoy the heights of French gastronomy in the warm and cosy atmosphere of *Le Baudelaire*. Indulge in infinitely elegant cuisine, and the perfect setting and décor.

Address: 8 Rue Duphot, 75001 Paris
Telephone: 01 42 60 34 12
Access: Métro Lines 18, 12, 14 *Madeleine* station, and Lines 1, 8, 12 *Concorde* station

Open: For lunch Monday to Friday from 12:30 to 14:30, and for dinner Monday to Saturday 19:30 to 22:30
Pricing: A la carte: €37 to €48.

LE PINXO

The restaurant was entrusted to Chef Alain Dutournier. It is in a modern and pleasant environment where you can enjoy various meal and recipes.
Address: 9 rue d'Alger, 75001 Paris
Telephone: 01 40 20 72 00
Access: Métro Line 1 *Tuileries* station
Open: Closed service. Open Monday to Friday from 12:15 to 14:15 and 19:00 to 22:00. Dinner service only on Saturday.
Pricing: A la Carte: €12 - €29.

2nd Arrondissement

BRASSERIE ROYAL VENDOME

A traditional Paris brasserie in the between *Opéra* and *Place Vendôme*. Here you will find a perfect mix of traditional French cuisine and modernism. From steak tartare to Norwegian salmon, everything is done with style.
Address: 26 Rue Danielle Casanova, 75002 Paris
Telephone: 01 42 61 48 36
Access: Métro Line 7 *Pyramides* station
Open: Every day. Lunch 12:00 to 16:00 and dinner 18:00 to 22:00
Pricing: Set Menu: €35. A la carte: €8.60 to €37.

LE MESTURET

Classic traditional French dishes, prepared the old fashioned way. A classic in Parisian style, décor, ambiance and wholesome food.
Address: 77 Rue de Richelieu, 75002 Paris
Telephone: 01 42 97 40 68
Access: Métro Line 3 *Quatre September* or *Bourse*
Open: Every day. Restaurant: Monday to Sunday from 12:00 to 23:00. Bar: Monday to Friday from 7:30 to 23:00, and Saturday and Sunday from 9:00 to 23:00.
Pricing: Menus: €26 - €31.50. A la carte: €8 to €17.10.

LE HELEM

From mezze to grilled dishes, *Le Helem* offers much more than just Lebanese food. Live entertainment and karaoke liven up the evenings at this extraordinary establishment.

Address: 164 Rue Saint Denis, 75002 Paris
Telephone: 01 40 39 09 69
Access: Métro Line 4 *Etienne Marcel*
Open: Every day. Open 12:00 to 15:30 and 19:30 to 23:00 from Monday to Saturday, and 12:00 to 15:30 on Sunday.
Pricing: Menus: €35 to €55. A la carte: €18 to €22.

3rd and 4th Arrondissements

BOFINGER

Since 1864, the Brasserie Bofinger has been delighting Parisians and visitors with traditional Alsatian cuisine. From "choucroute" and seafood choucroute to black pudding, a taste of France at its best.

Address: 5-7 Rue de la Bastille, 75004 Paris
Telephone: 01 42 72 87 82
Access: Métro Lines 1, 5 & 8 *Bastille* station
Open: Monday to Friday 12:00 to 15:00 and 18:30 to 00:00, Saturdays 12:00 to 15:30 and 18:30 to 00:00, and Sundays 12:00 to 23:00
Pricing: A la carte: €25 to €89.

LE CAFE BEAUBOURG

Enjoy the sights and buzz of the *Centre Pompidou* from the 200-seat terrace located opposite this icon.

Address: 100, Rue Saint Martin, 75004 Paris
Telephone: 01 48 87 63 96
Access: Métro Lines 1, 4, 7, 10, 11 and 14 *Châtelet* station / Lines 10 and 11 *Rambuteau* station
Open: Every day from 8:30 to 20:30
Pricing: Brunch: €23 to €25. Lunch and dinner menus: €30 to €60. A la carte: €9 to €21.

5th and 6th Arrondissements

L'ALCAZAR

A restaurant and bar with warm and elegant décor, a 12m high glass dome, and fine dining.

Address: 62 Rue Mazarine, 75006 Paris

Telephone: 01 53 10 19 99

Access: Métro Lines 4 & 10 *Odéon* station / RER Line B *St Michel* station

Open: 7 days a week from 12:00 to 14:30 and 19:00 to 23:30.

Pricing: Lunch set menus are priced at €22, €32 and €40. A la carte dishes from € 22. The dinner set menu is priced at €44 or à la carte dishes from € 22.

AUX CHARPENTIERS

Authentic French food in a 1930's decor, friendly and warm atmosphere.

Address: 10 Rue Mabillon, 75006 Paris

Telephone : 01 43 26 30 05

Access: Métro Line 10 *Mabilon* station, Line 4 *Saint-Germain-Des-Près* station and Lines 10 & 12 *Sèvres Babylone* station

Open: 7 days a week from 12:00 to 15:00 and 19:00 to 23:00

Pricing: Set menu priced at €20 for lunch and €30 for dinner. A la carte dishes from €20 to €60.

BRASSERIE LIPP

A standard in Parisian life, Brasserie Lipp has been the meeting point of famous politicians and writers since 1880. A must on a trip to Paris, so that you can say you have been there.

Address: 151 Boulevard Saint-Germain, 75006 Paris

Telephone: 01 45 48 53 91

Access: Métro Line 4 *Saint Germain-des-Près* station

Open: Every day. From 8:30am to 1:00am

Pricing: A la carte: €8.90 to €37.

7ᵗʰ Arrondissement

LE 122

Tradition meets contemporary in a light and trendy setting. Le 122 is fine and innovative dining at its best.

Address: 122 Rue de Grenelle, 75007 Paris
Telephone: 01 45 56 07 40
Access: Métro Line 12 *Solférino* station and Line 13 *Varenne* station
Open: For lunch Monday to Friday from 12:00 noon to 14:00, and for dinner Monday to Friday from 20:00 to 22:00
Pricing: Lunch set menu: €22. A la carte: €12 to €46.

L'ATELIER 197

A taste of Italy in the heart of Paris. Fresh food, from seafood to meat. The menu changes daily according to the availability at the market.

Address: 197 Rue de Grenelle, 75007 Paris
Telephone: 01 45 51 53 41
Access: Métro Line 8 *Ecole Militaire* station
Open: Every day from 12:00 to 22:30
Pricing: Brunch: €29. Menus: €14 to €22. A la carte: €12 to €18.

LES COCOTTES

The owner, star chef Christian Constant serves all the dishes in cast iron pots or glasses. Modern decor and tasty food at reasonable prices.

Address: 135 Rue Saint-Dominique, 75007 Paris
Telephone: 01 45 50 10 28
Access: Every day from 12:00 to 23:00.
Open: Métro Line 8 *Ecole Militaire* station
Pricing: Menus: €23 to €50. A la Carte: €25 to €30.

L'AFFRIOLE

The creative cuisine is always different and tasty in this lively bar in the 7th arrondissement. The moderate prices are a safe bet. The friendly service combines a nice atmosphere with a contemporary space, but be warned: its small size and popularity make it hard to be booked in.

Address: 17 Rue Malar, 75007 Paris
Telephone: 01 44 18 31 33
Access: Métro Line 8 *La Tour-Maubourg* station / RER Line C *Pont de l'Alma*
Open: Closed Sunday and Monday. Open Tuesday to Saturday from 12:15 to 14:30 and 19:15 to 22:30
Pricing: Set menus: €19 to €55.

8th Arrondissement

LE BŒUF SUR LE TOIT

This restaurant features an Art Déco style, fine food, a bright and airy dining room, and a real Parisian feel and atmosphere. Regular entertainment and live jazz is offered.

Address: 34 Rue du Colisée, 75008 Paris

Telephone: 01 53 93 65 55

Acccess: Métro Line 9 Saint Philippe du Roule station, Line 13 Miromesnil station, Lines 1 & 9 Franklin Roosevelt station / RER A Charles de Gaulle Etoile station

Open: Daily from 12:00 to 15:00 and 19:00 to 23:00 (midnight on Fridays and Saturdays)

Pricing: Set menus are €31 to €38. A la carte dishes from €24.50.

LA BASTIDE BLANCHE

Mediterranean food with a French flair, in a convivial and elegant setting, with an accent on fish and seafood.

Address: 1 Boulevard de Courcelles, 75008 Paris

Telephone: 01 40 08 08 25

Access: Métro Lines 1 & 3 *Villiers* station

Open: 12:00 to 15:00 and 19:00 to 23:00

Pricing: Brunch (All you can eat buffet) €29, children under 12: €15. Set menu (weekdays): €17.50, children under 12: €10.50. A la carte €17 to €28.

MARIUS & JANETTE

Fish and Seafood fine dining. Fresh Oysters, sustainable fish, in a warm and refined décor make this place a must visit.

Address: 4 Avenue George V, 75008 Paris

Telephone: 01 47 23 41 88

Access: Métro Line 1 *George V* station

Open: Daily from 12:00 to 15:00 and 19:00 to 23:00

Pricing: Set seafood menu: €48. A la carte: €24 to €60.

TANTE LOUISE

Traditional Parisian "bistro" style and décor, with wholesome French cuisine.

Address: 41 Rue Boissy d'Anglas, 75008 Paris

Telephone: 01 42 65 06 85

Access: Métro Lines 1, 8 & 12 *Concorde* station

Open: Daily from 12:00 to 14:00 and 19:00 to 22:30

Pricing: Set menus: €29 to €39. A la carte: €29 to €80.

BRASSERIE MOLLARD

A true Parisian tradition since its opening in 1865, this establishment has kept its *"cachet"* (character) and French elegance through various renovations and post-war reconstructions. A piece of history in the heart of Paris.

Address: 115 Rue Saint Lazare, 75008 Paris

Telephone: 01 46 33 69 75

Access: Métro Lines 3, 12, 13 & 14 – *Saint Lazare* station and Lines 3 & 9 – *Havre-Caumartin* station / RER Line A *Auber* station and Line B *Haussman Saint-Lazare* station

Open: Every day from noon to 00:30.

Pricing: 3-course set menu: € 35. A la carte: €12 to €49.

9ᵗʰ to 13ᵗʰ Arrondissements

LES COMEDIENS

Located in the heart of the theatre district, and modern and retro at the same time, *Les Comédiens* offers refined gastronomy, served with an artistic flair.

Address: 1, Rue de la Trinité, 75009 Paris

Telephone: 01 40 82 95 9

Access: Métro Line 12 *Trinité* station

Open: Open for lunch Monday to Friday from 12:00 noon to 14:30, and open for dinner Tuesday to Saturday from 19:00 to 23:00.

Pricing: A la carte €15 to €34. No set menus, the dishes change daily according to availability at markets.

BRASSERIE FLO

In an authentic setting dating from the 19th century, Brasserie FLO plunges you into the heart of Alsace and its gastronomy.

Address: 7 Cour des Petites Ecuries, 75010 Paris

Telephone: 01 47 70 13 59

Access: Métro Line 4 Chateau d'Eau or Strasbourg Saint Denis stations

Open: Every day. Sunday to Thursday from 12:00 to 15:00 and 19:00 to 23:00. Friday and Saturday from 12:00 to 15:00 and 19:00 to 00:00.

Pricing: Menus: €28.50 to €34.50. A la carte: €21 to €39.90. Takeaway available.

LE CHATEAUBRIAND

A trendy bistro that serves tasty, inventive and refined cuisine in a relaxed atmosphere.

Address: 129 Avenue Parmentier, 75011 Paris

Telephone: 01 43 57 45 95

Access: Métro Line 11 *Goncourt* station

Open: 19:30 to 23:00 (reservations are mandatory)

Pricing: One menu: €70

VIN ET MAREE – MAINE

Seafood and fresh oyster specialists with a specialised wine list. Takeaway is available, from single dishes to platters.

Address: 108 Avenue du Maine, 75014 Paris

Telephone: 01 43 20 29 50

Access: MétroLine 13 *Gaité* station

Open: Daily from 12:00 to 14:00 and 19:00 to 22:30 (23:00 on Fridays and Saturdays)

Pricing: Set seafood menus: €26 to €42. A la carte: €19.50 to €42.

LA COUPOLE

Emblem of Paris, this legendary Brasserie was *the place* where artists and writers used to gather. It has certainly kept its feel and atmosphere.

Address: 102 Boulevard du Montparnasse, 75014 Paris

Telephone: 01 43 20 14 20

Access: Métro Line 4 *Vavin* station

Open: Tuesday to Saturday from 12:00 to 00:00, and Sunday and Monday from 12:00 to 23:00.

Pricing: Menus: €31 to €38. Children's menu (4 to 12 yrs): €14.50. A la carte €22 to €42.

15th and 16th Arrondissements

LA PETITE BRETAGNE

For over 100 years, this bistro-type restaurant has been offering quality and tradition. From *andouillette* to *canard* (duck), you will get a true taste of France.

Address: 20 Rue du Cotentin, 75015 Paris

Telephone: 01 43 20 96 66

Access: Métro Line 13 *Gaité* station

Open: For lunch Saturday and Sunday from 12:00 to 15:30. Open daily for dinner from 19:00 to 23:30.

Pricing: Set menus: €13.50 to €15.50. A la carte: €22 to €45.

VICTOR

Fresh food with an emphasis on flavour. From accommodating old classics to unusual dishes, everything here is innovative.

Address: 101bis Rue Laniston, 75016 Paris
Telephone: 01 47 27 55 07
Access: Métro Line 2 *Pigalle* station
Open: Closed Sunday and Monday. Open for lunch Tuesday to Saturday from 12:00 to 14:00. Open for dinner Tuesday to Saturday from 19:00 to 22:30.
Pricing: Set menu: € 29. A la carte: €12 to €24.

17th Arrondissement

LE BALLON DES TERNES

French Brasserie offering a wide variety of traditional French cuisine, and seafood in an Art Deco décor.

Address: 103 Avenue des Ternes, 75017 Paris
Telephone: 01 45 74 17 98
Access: Métro Line 1 *Porte Maillot* station / RER Line C *Porte Maillot* station
Open: Daily. Lunch from 12:00 to 15:30, and dinner from 19:00 to 23:55.
Pricing: A la carte €7.50 to €69.

AU PETIT MARGUERY – RIVE DROITE

A famous chef, a unique approach to cooking and twists on traditional cuisine combine to make this establishment an explosive cocktail of elegance and refinement.

Address: 64 Avenue des Ternes, 75017 Paris
Telephone: 01 45 74 16 66
Access: Métro Line 2 *Ternes* station
Open: Daily. Lunch from 12:00 noon to 14:30, and dinner from 19:00 to 22:30
Pricing: Lunch set menus: €19.90 to €29. Dinner set menus: €31 to €37. Children's set menu: €16.

LE P'TIT MUSSET

Quality food, a wide and interesting menu, reasonable prices and attentive service make this one of our favourites places to dine in the 17th arrondissement.

Address: 132 Rue Cardinet, 75017 Paris

Telephone: 01 42 27 36 78

Access: Métro Line 2 *Rome* station

Open: For lunch: Monday to Friday from 12:00 to 14:15. For dinner: Monday to Saturday from 19:30 to 21:30.

Pricing: A la carte: €11 to €23.

L'AROME

Admire the open kitchen in this award-winning restaurant, as you watch the chef prepare outstanding dishes that will tantalise your taste buds. This restaurant is for the gourmet enthusiast wanting to experience something different, and awaken their senses. A full wine list is available, and the *"sommelier"* (wine specialist) will advise you on how to match your wine to your dish.

Address: 3 Rue Saint Philippe du Roule, 75008 Paris

Telephone: 01 42 25 55 98

Access: Métro Line 9 *Saint Philippe du Roule* station

Open: For lunch Monday to Friday from 12:00 to 14:00, and for dinner Monday to Friday from 19:30 to 21:30

Pricing: Lunch set menus: €59 to €159. Dinner set menus: €99 to €155.

18th Arrondissement

MIROIR

With a glass ceiling in the back, this bistro provides fresh and seasonal delights. The *Cave* (the cellar) is operated by the same people and located over the road. There you can choose a wine to take home or drink it right there.

Address: 94 Rue des Martyrs, Paris, 75018

Telephone: 01 46 06 50 73

Access: Metro Line 12 *Abbesses* station

Open: Daily from 12:00 to 14:00 and 19:30 to 22:00

Pricing: Set menus: €18 at lunch and €32 in the evening. A la carte: from €32.

Unique Dining Experiences
LES BATEAUX PARISIENS

Enjoy a dinner-cruise on one of the famous "Bateaux Mouche" boats that travel effortlessly up and down the Seine river.

Address: Port de la Bourdonnais, 75007 Paris

Telephone: 01 76 64 79 50

Access: Métro Line 6 *Bir Hakeim* station, Line 6 *Trocadéro* station, Line 9 *Champ de Mars – Tour Eiffel* / RER Line C *Champ de Mars – Tour Eiffel*

Open: Various departure times throughout the day. Enquire via telephone or at the physical location. Also see www.bateauxparisiens.com/dinner-cruise-paris.html.

Pricing: Set menus: €57 to €89. Children's set menus: €34.

LE COSTAUD DES BATIGNOLLES

A modern art gallery is the setting for this fun and convivial restaurant. Vintage furniture, an open kitchen, flavoursome food and welcoming staff make this place a must visit. A unique experience.

Address: 10 Rue Brochant, 75017 Paris

Telephone: 06 82 82 89 82

Access: Métro Line 13 *Brochant* station, Line 2 *Rome* station

Open: Closed Sundays and Mondays. Open for lunch Saturday only from 12:00 to 14:00. Open for dinner Tuesday to Saturday from 19:30 to 22:30.

Pricing: Set menu: €28 to €33. A la carte: €9 to €27.

LA TABLE DES GOURMETS

Classic traditional French cuisine served in the unusual setting of a 12th century chapel. An incredible setting for a unique experience.

Address: 14 Rue des Lombards, 75004 Paris
Telephone: 01 40 27 00 87
Access: Métro Lines 1 and 11 *Hotel de Ville* station
Open: Closed Sunday and Monday. Open for lunch Tuesday to Saturday from 12:00 to 14:00. Open for dinner Tuesday, Thursday, Friday and Saturday from 19:30 to 22:00.
Pricing: Set menus: €18 to €38. A la carte: €12 to €28.

LE CHARDENOUX

Opened in 1908, *Le Chardenoux* is one of the last true Parisian bistros registered as a historic monument. It was created by the family of the same name originally from *Lozère* who bought it in the early 20th century. Taken over in 2009 by Chef Cyril Lignac, it now honours French specialities. There are two big aims here: the respect for tradition and the use of local products.
Address: 1 rue Jules Vallès, 75011 Paris
Telephone: 01 43 71 49 52
Access: Métro Line 9 *Charonne* station
Open: Daily from 12:00 to 14:30 and 19:00 to 23:00
Pricing: Set menus: €22 to €39

Paris Nightlife

Paris is known for its class and this exudes even well into the night. Explore paris' nightlife hotspots here, including clubs and bars.

VIP ROOM

This spot is no less than 1000m² in size, organised into three areas: a lounge bar, a restaurant and the dance floor. The club, owned by the famous DJ Jean-Roch, is one of the finest in Paris.

Address: 188 bis rue de Rivoli 75001 Paris
Telephone: 01 80 96 02 00
Opening times: Monday to Saturday, 00:00 to 05:00
District: Louvre
Access: Métro Lines 1 & 7 *Palais Royal – Louvre* station / Bus 21, 27, 39, 48, 67, 68, 69, 72, 81, 95, Balabus

THE BARON

Open all night long, Le Baron is *the* trendy bar and club in *Avenue Marceau*, filled with stars and expensive drinks. This former strip club swapped its old image for a much more glorious reputation. Share a bottle with international stars, invite a supermodel onto the dance floor, and discuss the latest winners of the Cannes Film Festival with a director. This is what *The Baron* is about.

Address: 6 Avenue Marceau, 75008 Paris
Telephone: 01 47 20 04 01
Opening times: 23:00 to 07:00
District: Champs Elysées
Access: Métro Line 9 *Alma – Marceau* station

THE BILLIONAIRE CLUB

The Billionaire Club is located close to the *Place de la Madeleine*, the place where Hip-hop fans are sure to revel. This is the place to be if you like hip-hop music and a great atmosphere.

Address: 8 Boulevard de la Madeleine 75008 Paris
Telephone: 06 15 30 00 46
Opening times: Friday to Sunday from 00:00 to 06:00
District: Opéra - Grands Boulevards
Access: Métro Lines 8, 12 & 14 *Madeleine* station

CLUB MATIGNON

An institution founded by the famous Costes brothers, the Matignon is two venues in one: a restaurant and a club. At the restaurant you can taste creative French cuisine, and at the club you can enjoy electro pop music.

Address: 3 Avenue Matignon, 75008 Paris
Telephone: 01 42 89 64 72
Opening times: Daily from 9:00 to 2:00
District: Champs Elysées
Access: Métro Lines 1 & 9 *Franklin D. Roosevelt* station

CHEZ REGINE

Chez Régine was created by the singer Régine in the 1970s. Home to the craziest and most eccentric parties, its intimate setting and history have made it a well-known location worldwide. The club is now managed by Addy Bakhtiar and Romain Dian who have given it a second lease of life, especially since its renovation in 2012.

Address: 49 rue de Ponthieu, 75008 Paris
Telephone: 06 20 25 85 11
Opening times: Thursday: 19:00 to 05:00; Friday and Saturday: 23:30 to 07:00
District: Champs Elysées
Access: Métro Lines 1 & 9 *Franklin D. Roosevelt* station

Bars in Paris

If you are looking for a more refined, laid-back experience than the nightclubs mentioned in the previous section, take a look at some of our favourite cocktail bars and places to go for a drink in Paris here.

LE BALLROOM DU BEEF CLUB

Opened in March 2012, the Ballroom of Beef Club is ideally located in the heart of Paris. In the basement of the Beef Club steakhouse, its access by a dark metal staircase is an unusual experience.

Created by the team of the Experimental Cocktail Club (in the 2nd district) this cocktail lounge's underground location guarantees a cosy atmosphere between retro and carved ceilings, plush sofas and a solid wood bar. On the menu, there are a wide selection of cocktails, between great classics and original creations, including the "Pondicherry Mule", the "Salers Smach" or the "Marilou". Ideal for a drink before going out or after dinner.

Address: 58 rue Jean-Jacques Rousseau, 75001 Paris
District: Châtelet - Les Halles
Open: Daily from 19:00 to 05:00
Telephone: 09 52 52 89 34
Métro: Line 4 Etienne Marcel or Les Halles station or Line 1 Louvre-Rivoli station

BAR LE MAGNIFIQUE

Behind a glossy black front without a sign, *The Magnificent* is an amazing bar, designed as a large apartment and located near to the Louvre Museum. A flamboyant decor in homage to the seventies, with leather armchairs, coffee tables, wallpaper, woodwork, fur and even wicker chairs in the smoking room. Sushi or tiramisu are the perfect accompaniments to high-end cocktails offered in this discreet and trendy bar frequented by a happy few in Paris. The place turns into a nightclub after midnight.

Address: 25 rue de Richelieu, 75001 Paris
District: Louvre
Open: Every day. From 19:00 to 04:00
Telephone: 06 11 07 06 69
Metro: Lines 1 & 7 *Palais Royal* or *Musée du Louvre* stations or Lines 7 & 14 *Pyramides* station

LITTLE RED DOOR

This cocktail bar opened in the *Carreau du Temple* district. It follows the establishments of a similar style in New York. There is no name on the front of the Little Red Door, so to enter, you must know where it is. There is a very "Alice in Wonderland" moment as what appears to be a small red door hides a loft environment behind it.

Stone walls, red brick patchwork, armchairs, contemporary colours and paintings greet customers in a cocooning atmosphere. Behind the bar, there are original cocktails that change regularly. You can even request a custom creation by explaining your taste and mood atot the bartender. Craft beers are also available, and snacks are offered in accordance with the drinks menu.

Address: 60 rue Charlot, 75003 Paris
District: Marais
Open: From Monday to Saturday. From 18:00 to 02:00. Closed Sundays.
Telephone: 01 42 71 19 32
Métro: Line 8 *Filles du Calvaire* and *Saint-Sébastien – Froissart* stations

GLASS

Glass is the new bar by the now famous Candelaria team.
In this new trendy address of *Pigalle*, the focus is on an original selection of cocktails invented by the team, and American beers rather than intentionally simple and cosy decoration. The menu offers blends of flavours (lambic, shisho, pineapple syrup house) and South American alcohol such as Mezcal and Pisco.

Rock music runs from 19:00, and a DJ set begins at 22:00 every evening. The bar also offers a small dance floor, and enough to fill small appetites with pickles and hotdogs, New York style. Friendly and with influential guests, Glass has everything to become one of the trendiest bars in the city.

Address: 7 rue Frochot, 75009 Paris
District: Montmartre - La Chapelle
Open: Every day. From 19:00 to 02:00
Telephone: 09 80 72 98 83
Métro: Lines 2 & 12 *Pigalle* station

ENTRÉE DES ARTISTES

This cocktail bar is located in one of Paris' most well known nightlife hotspots, between *Rue Oberkampf* and *Place de La République*, just behind the *Cirque d'Hiver*. The small size of the bar makes it intimate, warm and relaxed. With its vintage decor and soft lighting, this place has become one of the trendiest bars in the area.

One reason for its success is the quality of the cocktails, some of which are very original. In the kitchen, chefs concoct elaborate and tasty finger food to accompany the cocktails.

Address: 8 rue de Crussol, 75010 Paris
District: Republic - East and North Stations
Open: Every day from 18:00 to 2:00
Telephone: 09 50 99 67 11
Métro: Line 8 *Filles du Calvaire* station

Paris Accommodation

Paris offers a wide variety of accommodation options for visitors, from bargain basement rooms to youth hostels, and apartments to deluxe hotels. Paris' accommodation is, however, notoriously expensive.

Choosing where to stay:
Paris' main attractions are located in its centre, with very few of them requiring you to travel outside this area. Therefore, if you favour being close to the attractions you should make sure to get a place to stay in the central arrondissements – these are: 1st, 4th, and the 5th and 6th – generally the closer you are to the river, the better you are located.

For more affordable accommodation you will want to travel out of the centre into one of the outer arrondissements. Be sure to read accommodation reviews online to avoid any particularly 'bad' neighbourhoods – the 18th and 19th arrondissements, for example.

We recommend staying *intra-muros* during your trip, as with public transport, you should be able to get anywhere in under 30 minutes: most trips are much shorter. The exception, of course, is if you will mainly be visiting the suburbs of the city.

Self-catering Apartments

For a family holiday or a longer stay, you might prefer the freedom offered by a self-catered apartment. Apartments generally provide much better value than hotel rooms, with a larger living space as well as low prices.

Hotel Family Residence 75
Single rooms and self-catering apartments sleeping up to three people.
Address: 23 Rue Fondary, 75015 Paris
Telephone: 01 43 92 42 42
Website: www.familyresidence75.com/index_en.html
Access: Métro Line 10 *Emile Zola* station, Line 6 *Dupleix* station, Line 8 *La Motte Piquet Grenelle* station / RER Line C *Champ de Mars-Tour Eiffel* station / Bus Line No. 42 *Rue Rouelle* stop
Budget: €80 to €120 per night.

Orion Paris Haussman
Serviced self-catering apartments, sleeping 1 to 4 guests.
Address: 2 Rue des Mathurins, 75009 Paris
Telephone: 01 42 68 59 00
Website: www.orion-international.net/en/rooms-services/
Access: Métro Lines 7 & 9 *Chaussée d'Antin* station, Lines 3 & 9 Havre
Caumartin station / RER Line A *Auber* station
Budget: €134 to €154 per night

Stay City Serviced Apartments
Self-catering apartments, serviced daily.
Address: 5-7 Passage Dubail, 75010 Paris
Telephone: 01 44 89 66 70
Website: www.staycity.com/paris/gare-de-lest-apartments/
Access: Métro Lines 4 & 5 *Gare de l'Est* station
Budget: €65 to €136 per night

A variety of websites regroup the various self-catering options in Paris, with a wide selection to choose from, including: **One Fine Stay** - www.onefinestay.com; **All Paris Apartments** - www.all-paris-apartments.com/en/paris-apartments; **House Trip** - www.housetrip.com/en/paris; **Paris Appartements** - www.paris-appartements-services.com/en/; **Only Apartments** - www.only-apartments.com; **Way to Stay** - www.waytostay.com; and **My Apartment Paris** - www.myapartmentparis.com.

Bed and Breakfast/Guest Houses/Apartment Rentals

Whether you are staying in Paris for one night or a few days, you might be looking for an accommodation system that is more flexible, has more of a "home feel", and to experience the "French lifestyle". If this is you, a guest house, bed and breakfast or even a room in a family's private house is ideal. Interact with the locals, get tips from them, and make new friends for life.

In order to ensure that you are booking in a legal and high-quality establishment, we have here a selection of organisations and websites that regroup the various options: **Chambres Hotes** - www.chambres-hotes.fr; **AirBnB** – www.airbnb.com/c/gdacosta16?s=8 (Use our special link for at least $25/£16/€23 off your first booking); **Hotes Qualite Paris -** www.hotesqualiteparis.fr; and **Chambre Ville -** www.chambre-ville.com.

Flat Exchange

This is a novel, very popular and friendly way of staying in a big city on a budget. If you want to visit Paris, and a Parisian would like to visit your city, then consider a flat exchange. That's when the other party will stay at your place, while you stay at theirs. Given the risk incurred in such an operation, ensure that you use a reputable website, and that all your transactions go through the organiser.

Also ensure that you lock up all your valuables and fragile items in a separate room unreachable to your "tenants", that your apartments and belongings are properly insured, and communicate with the other party as much as you can prior to the exchange.

Follow the rules of the chosen organiser's website carefully and you are in for a wonderful experience.

A list of sample websites includes: **Love Home Swap** - www.lovehomeswap.com; **Guest to Guest** - www.guesttoguest.com/en/; **Home for Home** - http://en.homeforhome.com; and **Intervac Home Exchange** - www.intervac-homeexchange.com.

Hotels

Paris hosts a wide variety of hotels, catering for all budgets.

The French Hotel Rating System:
Since 2009, France has operated a government-operated hotel rating system. Unlike some other hotel rating systems around the world that measure factors such as amenities, customer service, cleanliness, location, accessibility, room views and size, the French system does not take all of these into account.

Instead, the French system is rather more objective than subjective. Rather than including factors like the quality of service, a list of amenities and facilities are used to determine a star rating. Therefore, your hotel will be rated based on the size of the rooms, whether reception staff can speak several languages, whether the hotel has air conditioning, and how many hours a day the reception is open. This means that customer service, decor and cleanliness, for example, are not taken into account when scoring a hotel.

Hotels are rated from 1-star locations (the most basic) to 5-star locations (the most luxurious), with exceptional places being awarded "Palace" status.

Note that the full '5-star' rating has only come into existence in the past few years and therefore there are still many world-class properties in the city that only have 4-star or 3-star ratings. Elsewhere these would be 5-stars. Equally, just because a hotel has a 4-star rating and has large rooms, does not mean it will be in an ideal location, have good customer service, or be spotless. We suggest reading online reviews of any hotels booked to help you decide.

How to book:
Online bookings always attract the best deals and discounts, so we have made a selection of our favourite booking websites to help you in your decision: Booking.com, Hotels.com, Hotels-Paris.fr and Trivago.co.uk.

Recommended places to stay:

Here is a selection of some of our recommended hotels in Paris. As always be sure to read online reviews and do research before booking in case they have changed since we last visited.

1st Arrondissement:

HOTEL LUMEN

Right in the middle of historical Paris, Hotel Lumen offers quality accommodation. From single rooms to suites, this elegant establishment will definitely add a touch of class to your stay.

Address: 15 Rue des Pyramides, 75001 Paris
Telephone: 01 44 50 77 00
Website: www.hotel-lumenparis.com
Rooms: €170 to €185
Suites: €298
Amenities: Satellite television, mini bar, wi-fi, air conditioning, hair dryer, lift, safe, concierge, restaurant, gym and meeting room
Nearby Attractions: *Musée du Louvre, Jardins des Tuileries* and *Place Vendôme*
Métro: Lines 7 & 14 *Pyramides* station / Line 1 *Tuileries* station

LE MELIA VENDOME

83 spacious and comfortable rooms, each elegantly decorated. From a single room to the Grand Suite, this establishment offers affordable luxury in the very heart of the City of Lights.

Address: 8 Rue Cambon, 75001 Paris
Telephone: 01 44 77 54 00
Website: www.melia.com/fr/hotels/france/paris/melia-vendome-boutique-hotel-fr/index.html
Rooms: €149 to €245
Amenities: Satellite television, mini bar, wi-fi, air conditioning, writing desk and bar
Nearby Attractions: *Jardin des Tuileries, Place Vendôme* and *Musée du Louvre*
Métro: Métro Line 1 *Concorde* station / RER Line A *Auber* station

HOTEL LE BURGUNDY

Personalised service, ultimate luxury and executive standards, this exceptional establishment welcomes business travellers, as well as honeymooning couples and families. Within a short walking distance of the main Paris attractions, the Burgundy Hotel will be your ideal base for a fulfilling stay in Paris.

Address: 6 Rue Duphot, 75001 Paris
Telephone: 01 42 60 34 12
Website: www.leburgundy.com/en
Rooms: €460 to €560
Suites: €700 to €2200
Amenities: Satellite television, mini bar, wi-fi, air conditioning, hair dryer, concierge, desk, spa, swimming pool, restaurant, bar, Lounge and events/seminars
Nearby Attractions: *Palais Royal, Opéra Garnier, Shopping* and *Champs Elysées*
Métro: Lines 8, 12 & 14 *Madeleine* station

6th Arrondissement:

TONIC HOTEL SAINT GERMAIN

In the heart of the 6th arrondissement, the Tonic Hotel Saint Germain welcomes you in a historical 17th century building. At this intimate and cosy hotel, you will be cocooned in your spacious and comfortable room. From single to family rooms and a top suite, there is a solution for everyone.

Address: 15 Rue des Quatre Vents, 75006 Paris
Telephone: 01 43 26 35 50
Website: www.hotelduglobeparis.com
Rooms: €72 to €87
Amenities: Underfloor heating/cooling, Satellite television, Private bathroom with shower or bath, Hairdryer, Safe, Mini Bar, 24/7 front desk and Wi-Fi
Nearby Attractions: *Musée du Luxembourg, Luxembourg Gardens* and *Eglise Saint Sulpice*
Métro: Métro Line 4 *Odéon* station / RER Line C *Saint Michel / Notre Dame* station

7th Arrondissement:

LE BELLECHASSE SAINT GERMAIN

Address: 8 Rue de Bellechasse, 75007 Paris
Telephone: 01 45 50 22 31
Website: www.lebellechasse.com
Rooms: €315 to €398
Amenities: Satellite television, Mini Bar, WiFi, Air conditioning, Hair Dryer and Concierge
Nearby Attractions: *Parc Monceau, Champ de Mars and Tour Eiffel, Invalides* and armour museum
Métro: Line 12 *Solférino* station and Line 13 *Varenne* station

HOTEL PONT ROYAL

From a classic room to the panoramic views from the top suite, wherever you are staying at the Pont Royal will provide you with luxury and comfort.

Address: 7 Rue Montalembert, 75007 Paris
Telephone: 01 42 84 70 00
Website: www.leshotelsduroy.com/fr/hotel-pont-royal
Rooms: €405 to €1200
Amenities: Satellite television, Mini Bar, WiFi, Air conditioning, Hair Dryer, Concierge, Desk, Restaurant and Bar, Lounge and Events/Seminars
Nearby Attractions: *Musée du Quai Branly, Champ de Mars, Tour Eiffel* and *Invalides*
Métro: Line 12 *Rue du Bac* station

8th Arrondissement:

HOTEL PARIS SAINT HONORE

Luxury in the heart of Paris at an affordable price. The romantic Hotel Saint Honoré welcomes you in elegantly decorated, warm, and cosy rooms. Dedicated staff are available 24/7, Paris is at your feet, and everything here is designed to make your stay in Paris as enjoyable as possible.

Address: 21 Rue Penthièvre, 75008 Paris
Telephone: 01 43 59 87 63
Website: http://www.paris-saint-honore.com
Rooms: €55 to €126
Amenities: Satellite television, Mini Bar, WiFi, Air conditioning, Hair Dryer, Lift and Safe
Nearby Attractions: *Arc de Triomphe, Palais de la Découverte* and *Parc Monceau*
Métro: Lines 9 & 13 *Miromesnil* station

HOTEL DU COLLECTIONNEUR

Get pampered in Parisian luxury, enjoy relaxing moments at the spa, savour a romantic dinner at the restaurant, rest in the luxurious bedding and take full advantage of your extremely spacious room or suite.

Address: 51-57 Rue de Courcelles, 75008 Paris
Telephone: 01 58 36 67 00
Website: www.hotelducollectionneur.com
Rooms: €259 to €432
Amenities: Satellite television, Mini Bar, Wi-Fi, Air conditioning, Hair Dryer, Lift, Safe, Concierge, Restaurant, Spa
Nearby Attractions: *Parc Monceau, Arc de Triomphe, Avenue des Champs Elysées*
Métro: Line 2 *Courcelles* station

HOTEL ROYAL MADELEINE

Luxury and simplicity in traditional Parisian style. Large and comfortable rooms, from single rooms to deluxe options. All rooms are elegantly decorated. Enjoy the vibe and atmosphere of the *Champs Elysées*, the shopping, and live like a Parisian!

Address: 29 Rue de l'Arcade, 75008 Paris
Telephone: 01 43 66 13 81
Website www.hotelroyalmadeleine.com/en/
Rooms: €107 to €229
Amenities: Satellite television, Mini Bar, WiFi, Air conditioning, Writing Desk and Bar
Nearby Attractions: *Palais de la Découverte, Arc de Triomphe, Parc Monceau* and *Eglise de la Madeleine*
Métro: Métro Lines 8, 12 & 14 *Madeleine* station

ROCHESTER CHAMPS ELYSEES

You will feel at ease at the cosy and warm Rochester Hotel. From your ultra comfortable room to the garden or the lounge, everything here is designed to facilitate your stay and make it one to remember.

Address: 92 Rue la Boétie, 75008 paris
Telephone: 01 56 69 69 00
Website: www.hrochester.com/en/page/4-star-hotel-paris-champs-elysees.2.html
Rooms: €195 to €395
Amenities: Satellite television, Mini Bar, WiFi, Air conditioning, Writing Desk and Bar
Nearby Attractions: *Palais de la Découverte, Arc de Triomphe, Parc Monceau* and *Eglise de la Madeleine*
Métro: Lines 1 & 9 *Franklin Roosevelt* station

SOFITEL PARIS FAUBOURG

The perfect location to relax after a long day visiting Paris, this establishment combines luxury, comfort, relaxation and tranquillity. The spacious and airy rooms are elegantly decorated and will make you feel at home.

Address: 15 Rue Boissy d'Anglas, 75008 Paris
Telephone: 01 44 94 14 14
Website: www.galahotels.com/en/Hotel/FRANCE_3/PARIS_5733/SOFITEL_PARIS_LE_FAUBOURG_125314/
Rooms: €149 to €245
Amenities: Satellite television, Mini Bar, WiFi, Air conditioning, Writing Desk and Bar
Nearby Attractions: Jardin des Tuileries, Place Vendôme and Musée du Louvre
Métro: Métro Line 1 *Concorde* station / RER Line A *Auber* station

16th Arrondissement:

HOTEL RAPHAEL

Set in an ideal location, with perfect views over Paris in the heart of all the luxury the city has to offer, the Raphael will leave you in awe. From standard rooms to suites, comfort and elegance are a priority here.

Address: 17 Avenue Kleber, 75016 Paris
Telephone: 01 53 64 32 00
Website: www.raphael-hotel.com/fr/hotel-5-etoiles-champs-elysees-site-officiel.php
Rooms: €485- €620
Suites: Prices not available at the time of writing
Amenities: Satellite television, Mini Bar, WiFi, Air conditioning, Hair Dryer, Concierge, Desk, Spa, Gym, Restaurant / Bar, Lounge and Events/Seminars
Nearby Attractions: *Jardin d'Acclimatation, Palais de Tokyo* and the maritime museum
Métro: Line 6 *Kléber* station

17th Arrondissement:

HOTEL DES BATIGNOLLES

A haven of peace and tranquillity in the big city, this establishment is ideal for visitors who want to sit back and relax after a long day of sightseeing. Rooms for 1, 2 or 3 guests.

Address: 26-28 Rue des Batignolles, 75017 Paris
Telephone: 01 43 87 70 40
Website: www.batignolles.com
Rooms: €56 - €70
Amenities: Satellite television, Private bathroom with shower or bath, Safe available at reception, Concierge, Wi-Fi and Free baby cot on request
Nearby Attractions: *Square des Batignolles, Parc Monceau* and a flower market
Métro: Line 2 *Place de Clichy* station / *Rome* station, Line 13 *Place de Clichy* station / *La Fourche* station

19ᵗʰ Arrondissement:

HOTEL CRIMEE

Recently renovated, you will find comfort, modernism, space and relaxing décor at the Hotel Crimée. Be cocooned in the heart of Paris. There are a variety of rooms accommodating 1 to 4 guests.

Address: 188 Rue de Crimée, 75019 Paris
Telephone: 01 40 36 75 29
Website: www.hotelcrimee.com
Rooms: €60 to €130
Amenities: Satellite television, Private bathroom with shower or bath, Common lounge, WiFi, Air conditioning, Hair Dryer and Lift
Nearby Attractions: *Cité des Sciences, Pont Levant at Rue de Crimée* and *Parc de la Villette*
Métro: Line 7 *Crimée* station

HOTEL CAMPANILE LA VILLETTE

Within walking distance of the *Parc de la Villette*, this hotel offers very good value for money, and the perfect place to stay for a family or while on a business trip. Single rooms, double rooms and family rooms are available.

Address: 147 / 151 Avenue des Flandres, 75019 Paris
Telephone: 01 44 72 46 46
Website: www.campanile.com/fr/hotels/campanile-paris-19-la-villette
Rooms: From €59
Amenities: Air conditioning, Satellite television, Private bathroom with shower, 24/7 front desk, WiFi, Lift, Disabled friendly, Restaurant/coffee shop, Meeting rooms and Garden
Nearby Attractions: *Cité des Sciences et de l'Industrie, Canal de l'Ourcq* and *Parc de la Villette*
Métro: Métro Line 7 *Crimée* station

Shopping

Paris is a shopper's heaven. From luxury and designer items to bargains and great sales, you are sure to find treasures to take home with you. Shops in Paris usually open between 9:00 and 10:00, and close at 19:00. Most shops are closed on Sundays (including most supermarkets), except in certain areas such as the *Champs Elysées* and other tourist spots.

The sale season is regulated in France, and the best moments to get bargains are during the summer and winter sales. The summer sales for 2016 run from 22nd June to 2nd August inclusive. The winter sales will run from end January to mid-February 2017 but exact dates were not available at the time of going to print.

If you are resident in a country outside of the European Union, you can get the TVA (sales tax) refunded at your point of departure, such as at the airport. Ensure you request a tax invoice for all purchases (ask for a "facture") and keep it with the items bought. Refunds are given for goods valued over €175 bought in the same store on the same day. Note that these items must still be in a "new" state when claiming your refund, so that new camera cannot be opened before you have it checked by customs.

Paris is filled with shops in every direction. Here are a selection of the main shopping areas.

1) Rue de Rivoli area
Along this lengthy street you will find *Le BHV Marais (Bazar de l'Hotel de Ville)* department store, where you will find everything from designer clothing to perfumes, jewellery or leather goods. Brands such as H&M, Zara, Desigual, and the Apple Store are present. Souvenir shops are located all along this street, too, selling French and Parisian souvenirs.

Where to shop in the area: *Rue de Rivoli, Rue du Faubourg Saint Antoine, Rue de la Verrière* and *Rue des Archives*

Métro: Line 1 *Saint Paul* station, Lines 1 & 11 *Chatelet* station, and Lines 1 & 7 *Palais Royal* station

2) Louvre, Tuileries, Champs Elysées areas

The *Louvre, Tuileries* and *Champs Elysées* areas are dedicated to luxury shopping. All the famous designers have boutiques on the Faubourg Saint Honoré (YSL, Hermès, Prada, etc...) and the Place Vendôme is the hub for jewellers such as Cartier, Lanvin, Gucci, etc... You do not have to be looking to buy these luxury items to stroll past these shops. The experience in itself is quite tantalising.

Where to shop in the area: *Rue de la Paix, Place Vendôme, Rue Faubourg Saint Honoré, Rue François 1er* and *Avenue Montaigne*

Métro: Line 1 *Concorde* station, Line 1 *Tuileries* station, Lines 1 & 9 *Franklin Roosevelt*, and Lines 1 & 7 *Palais Royal*

3) Le Marais

If you are looking for something different and unusual, as well as art galleries, the Marais is for you. This area is very popular with modern young designers and artists, and buzzes even on Sundays. There is always something happening in the Marais. For shoes, art, and fashion, this area is not to be missed!

Where to shop in the area: *Rue Sévigné, Rue de Turenne, Place des Vosges, Rue des Francs-Bourgeois, Rue des Rosiers* and *Rue Saint Croix de la Bretonnerie*

Métro: Line 1 *Saint Paul* Station

4) Saint Germain des Près

Variety characterises shopping in the *Saint Germain des Près* district. Historically a favourite place for intellectuals and reading fans, the area is now home to a wide range of shops and boutiques offering everything from designer and luxury clothing to second hand books.

Where to shop in the area: *Boulevard Saint-Germain, Rue de Rennes, Rue de Sèvres, Rue du Bac, Boulevard Raspail* and *Rue Saint André des Arts*

Métro: Line 4 *Saint-Germain-des-Près* station, and Line 10 *Sèvres-Babylone* staion

5) Opéra – Chaussée d'Antin

Heaven for big shoppers, this area is home to the famous *Printemps* and *Galeries Lafayette* department stores, which are as much shopping zones as they are architectural, historical and cultural monuments.

Where to shop in the area: *Rue de Caumartin, Boulevard Haussmann* and *Rue Scribe*

Métro: Line 7 *Chaussée d'Antin* station, and Lines 3 & 9 *Havre-Caumartin* station

6) 14th Arrondissement

The perfect area for bargain shopping, the 14th Arondissement hosts a variety of factory shops, including designer outlets and end of season sale shops. Enjoy massive discounts on luxury merchandise, from clothing to leather goods, perfumes, etc…

Where to shop in the area: *Rue d'Alésia* and *Boulevard du Général Leclerc*

Métro: Line 4 *Alésia* station

7) The famous second hand booksellers along the Seine River

Over 300,000 second hand (and new) books are sold along a 3km stretch of the river, making a leisurely riverside walk even better.

Following a 500-year-old tradition of travelling booksellers, these guardians of history and culture have settled along the Seine River, and are a Paris feature not to be missed. Browse, chat with the sellers amongst their famous green booths, and have a stroll while admiring the view.

Location: On the right bank from *Pont Marie* to *Quai François Mitterrand*, and on the left bank from *Quai de la Tournelle* to *Quai Voltaire*

Open: From 11:30 to sunset, 7 days a week

Métro: Line 7 *Pont Marie* station, and Lines 1 & 7 *Palais Royal – Musée du Louvre* station

8) The famous « Marché aux Puces de Saint Ouen »

The fourth most visited tourist attraction in France, and the biggest antiques and second hand goods market in the world. The *Saint Ouen* flea market is a heaven for antique hunters as well as a treat for visitors. Walk amongst the hundreds of sellers, browse the massive selection of goods, from old radios to antique couches, and enjoy the unique ambiance and atmosphere.

Opening hours: Saturday 9:00 to 18:00 / Sunday 10:00 to 18:00 / Monday 11:00 to 17:00. Reduced activity between 1st and 15th of August.

Métro: Line 4 *Porte de Clignancourt* station, and Line 13 *Garibaldi* station

9) Les Quatre Temps

Les Quatre Temps, located inside the *La Défense* towers, is a big traditional shopping centre where you will find a wide variety of shops, boutiques, chain stores, restaurants and cinemas.

Opening hours: Monday to Sunday from 10:00 to 20:00. Some shops are closed on Sundays.

Métro: Line 1 *La Défense* or *Chateau de Vincennes* station / RER Line *A La Défense* station

10) Buying souvenirs in Paris

All monuments and museums have a souvenir shop where one can buy souvenirs and related items. However, these shops can be very costly. Do not forget to browse the numerous shops around the attractions, where you will find the same items much cheaper. *Rue de Rivoli* is famous for its souvenir shops, where you will find everything from t-shirts to fridge magnets.

Do not buy from the street sellers, as you will be supporting an illegal trade. The only reason these street sellers are everywhere in Paris is because people keep supporting their trade.

Unusual Places to Visit

Once you have visited the big name attractions, and eaten in the finest restaurants in the city, you may want to take in one of Paris' more unique locations. This chapter takes a look at some of our favourite unusual places to visit in the city.

MUSEE DES EGOUTS DE PARIS (Paris sewage system network Museum)

2500kms long, the Paris sewage system is a complicated network of canals and caves originally built in 1200. This visit will take you along a secured and sanitised part of this incredible network, where you will learn how the system was first built and how it is maintained. Experience a unique way to visit Paris.

Address: Pont de l'Alma, Rive Gauche - Opposite 93 Quai d'Orsay, 75007 Paris
Telephone: 01 53 68 27 81
Access: Métro Line 9 *Marceau* station / RER Line C *Pont de l'Alma*
Rates: Adults - €4.40, Students & children 6 to 16 years old - €3.60
Open: Saturday to Wednesday year-round. Closed Thursdays and Fridays. Open from 11:00 to 16:00 from October to April, and from 11:00 to 17:00 from May to September.
Additional information: The visit lasts about 1 hour and is suitable for children. There are 42 steps to get inside, 42 steps to go back up. There is no lift/elevator. Visitors who experience pulmonary problems or claustrophobia are warned to exercise caution and obtain medical advice prior to visiting.

PERFUME MUSEUM

Set in a beautiful and elegant historic building, this perfume museum takes you on a journey of discovery of the history of French perfumery through the ages.

Address: 9 Rue Scribe, 75009 Paris
Telephone: 01 47 45 04 56
Access: Métro Lines 3, 7 & 8 *Opéra* station / RER Line A *Auber* station
Rates: Free entry
Open: From 9:00 to 18:00 Monday to Saturday, and 9:00 to 17:00 on Sunday and Public Holidays.

MUSEUM OF MAGIC

A history of magic from the 18th century to today. Guided by a magician, you will learn the origins of illusion and magic, and understand accessories. Finally, the captivating magic show topping your visit will leave you dazzled.

Address: 11 Rue Saint Paul, 75004 Paris
Telephone: 01 42 72 13 26
Access: Métro Lines 1, 4, 5 & 7 *Saint Paul, Bastille* or *Sully-Morand* stations
Rates: Adults - €9. Children 3 to 12 - €7.
Open: Wednesday, Saturday and Sunday from 14:00 to 19:00

MAISON DEYROLLE (Museum of Strange things)

Curiosities, odd objects, taxidermy, the most unusual items can be seen in this museum that doubles up as a shop. Here you can browse freely and be transported into the universe of this 200-year-old house of curiosities.

Address: 46 Rue du Bac, 75007 Paris
Telephone: 01 42 22 30 07
Access: Métro Line 12 *Rue du Bac* station
Rates: Free entry
Open: Monday from 10:00 to 13:00 and 14:00 to 19:00, and Tuesday to Saturday from 10:00 to 19:00. Closed Sunday.

MUSEE DU VIN (Wine Museum)

Experience a journey of discovery in the traditional French craft of winemaking. The visit takes you through 15th century caves, where you will learn about the history of wine, the various methods of winemaking, as well as the evolution of equipment and accessories. After your visit, why not have a nice lunch at the adjoining restaurant, where you will be able to taste more wine and apply your newfound wine matching skills?

Address: Siège du Grand Orient de France, 16 Rue Cadet, 75009 Paris
Telephone: 01 45 25 63 26
Access: Métro Line 6 *Passy* station / RER Line C *Champ de Mars-Tour Eiffel* station
Rates: Entrance fee - €10, Wine tasting (1 glass) - €5
Open: Tuesday to Saturday from 10:00 to 18:00. Closed Sundays and Mondays.

Things to do with the kids

Although Paris is often seen as a good destination to go as a couple, there are also plenty of opportunities to keep the younger members of the family amused too. Here is a small selection of the activities the city has on offer. Remember that there are many other attractions that will appeal to children – you can read about these in the main attractions chapter.

LE JARDIN D'ACCLIMATATION

This immense park in the heart of Paris offers a wide variety of fun and educational activities for kids. Pony or camel rides, river cruises, farm animals, mini-golf, kids workshops (some of them held in English) and more are available to keep the children entertained.

Address: Bois de Boulogne, 75016 Paris
Telephone: 01 40 67 90 85
Métro: Line 1 *Les Sablons* station. Mini train available from *Porte Maillot* to the entrance of the park
Rates: Entry for adults and children over 3 years is €3, Children under 3 years and disabled persons: Free. Attractions: €2.90 per attraction. Possibility to buy tickets in bulk, from €35 for 15 tickets to €90 for 50 tickets. Train from Porte Maillot: Return trip €2.90 per person.
Open: Every day of the year. From April to September, the park is open from 10:00 to 19:00 daily, with a late closing at 22:00 on Fridays. From October to March, the park is open from 10:00 to 18:00 Mondays to Thursdays, 10:00 to 22:00 on Fridays, and 10:00 to 19:00 on the weekend.

PUPPET SHOWS – Jardin du Luxembourg

A delightful and timeless spectacle, these puppet shows will delight children as well as their parents. The shows are in French but trust your children to understand and recognise the classic stories told. From Little Red Riding Hood to The Three Little Pigs, such classics never fail to entertain.

Address: Jardin du Luxembourg, 75006 Paris
Telephone: Programmes: 01 43 26 46 47. Information: 01 43 29 50 97
Métro: Line 4 *Vavin* station, and Line 12 *Notre Dame des Champs* station
Rates: Tickets are €4.80 per person
Open: Wednesday, Saturday, Sunday and Public Holidays. Programs change regularly so call to enquire
Additional information: No reservations necessary. Arrive 20 to 30 minutes before the start of the show. Shows are about 40 minutes long.

DISNEYLAND PARIS

Not only for children, adults can have fun too at Disneyland Paris. From magical journeys through the various attraction to parades, character meets and fireworks there is fun for everyone. It can take several days to see all the resort has to offer. For a full 188-page guide to Disneyland Paris written by an ex-employee, check out *The Independent Guide to Disneyland Paris 2016*, sold separately.

Address: Disneyland Paris, 77777 Marne –la-Vallee
Telephone: 0825 30 0530
Website: www.disneylandparis.com
Open: 365 days a year. Opening hours vary depending on the season from 10:00am to 6:00pm in low season to 10:00am to 11:00pm in high season.
Rates: Different rates apply depending on how far in advance tickets are purchased. Gate prices are €75 for a one-park, one-day adult ticket and €90 for a two-park, one-day adult ticket. Children prices are a few euros cheaper. Discounts are available online and in advance. Children under 3 go free.
Access: Shuttles from airports to the park's entrance via www.magicalshuttle.fr / Daily shuttles from *Paris Gare du Nord, Opéra, Madeleine, Châtelet* / RER Line A *Marne la Vallee – Chessy* station (40 minutes from central Paris) / *Marne la Vallee – Chessy* TGV Station

PALAIS DE LA DECOUVERTE – Science Museum

From Leonardo Da Vinci's inventions and discoveries to the first steps on the moon, to modern technology, the *Palais de la Découverte* is a must-see. All aspects of science are presented and explained in a fun, interactive and entertaining way with activities for adults, as well as children.

Address: Avenue F. D. Roosevelt, 75008 Paris
Telephone: 01 44 13 17 35
Métro: Lines 1 & 13 *Champs Elysées - Clémenceau* station, and Lines 1 & 9 *Franklin D. Roosevelt* station / RER Line C *Invalides* station
Rates: Adults over 25 - €9, Children and students under 25 - €7, Children under 6 go free
Open: Tuesday to Saturday from 9:30 to 18:00, and Sunday and Public Holidays from 10:00 to 19:00. Closed on Mondays and on 1st January, 1st May, 14th July and 25th December.

Thanks and acknowledgements:

If you have made it this far, thank you very much for reading everything – we hope this guide has made a big difference to your vacation and that you have found tips that will save you time, money and hassle! Remember to take this guide with you whilst you are visiting the city.

To contact us, please use the 'Contact Us' form on our website at http://www.independentguidebooks.com/contact-us/. If you have any corrections, feedback about any element of the guide, or a review of an attraction or restaurant - send us a message and we will get back to you!

If you have enjoyed this travel guide you will want to check out **The Independent Guide to London 2016** and **The Independent Guide to New York City 2016**. We also have theme park travel guides, including **The Independent Guide to Disneyland Paris 2016**, **The Independent Guide to Universal Orlando 2016, The Independent Guide to Disneyland 2016**, and **The Independent Guide to Walt Disney World 2016**. All of these travel guides are available in both print and digital formats.

Have a fantastic time in Paris!

Photo credits:

The following photos have been used in this guide under a Creative Commons license. Thank you to:

Eiffel Tower at sunset in-book – Sam Valadi; Notre-Dame de Paris - William John Gauthier; Avenue des Champs-Elysées - Christian Scheja; Musée d'Orsay – David Loong; Arc de Triomphe – Arek Olek; Musée de L'Orangerie – LWYang (Flickr); Jardin du Luxembourg – David McSpadden; Sainte-Chapelle – Gary Ullah; Jardin des Tuileries – Jean-Pierre; Palais Royal – Chris Yunker; La Conciergie - Guillaume Speurt; Musée du Louvre – Dennis Jarvis; Place des Vosges – Peter Dutton; Ile de la Cité – Edgardo W. Olivera; Musée Carnavalet – Nelson Minar; Disneyland Paris - 'Doggettx' (Flickr); Musée Picasso – 'Amaya M.G.M.' (Flickr); Ile Saint Louis – Coralie Ferreira; Hotel de Ville – Edwin Lee; The Panthéon – 'Besopha' (Flickr); Musée de Cluny – Karen Green; Jardin des Plantes – Tom Hilton; Musée Rodin – 'Oh Paris' (Flickr); Musée Marmottan Monet - Pierre Mondain-Monval; Musée de l'armée – 'Son of Groucho' (Flickr); Musée du Quai Branly – Virginia Manso; Pont Alexandre III – Darek Rusin; Place de la Concorde – m-louis (Flickr); Palais Garnier – Rog01 (Flickr); Père Lachaise Cemetry – Jim Linwood; Cité des Sciences – 'sacratomato_hr' (Flickr); Musée Jacquemart-André – David McSpadden; Parc des Buttes Chaumont – Chris Lancaster; Petit Palais – Jean-Louis Zimmermann; Grand Palais – Dennis Jarvis; Bateaux Mouches – David McSpadden; Parc Monceau – 'ParisSharing' (Flickr); Monmartre Cemetery – 'Eric@Focus' (Flickr); Eglise de la Madeleine – Dennis Jarvis; Place de la Bastille – Jean-Louis Zimmermann; Musée Grévin – Mark C-F; Opéra Bastille – Carles Tomás Martí; Notre Dame de Lorette – Connie Ma; Canal Saint Martin – 'Hotzeplotz' (Flickr); Zoo de Vincennes – 'Rog01' (Flickr); The Catacombes – Passion Leica; Paris Modern Art Museum – Mark B. Schlemmer; Musée national de la marine – Jean-Pierre Dalbéra; Musée Jeu de Paume – Susan Sermoneta; Bois de Boulogne – Andrea Anastasakis; Chateau Versailles – Dennis Jarvis; Eiffel Tower (cover) – Jiuguang Wang; Eiffel Tower at sunset (cover) – Moyan Brenn; Metro sign (cover) – Pedro Ribeiro Simões; Parisian street (cover) – Moyan Brenn; and The Louvre (cover) – Dennis Jarvis.

Printed in Great Britain
by Amazon